THE DATING GAME: HOW *HE* PLAYS IT

*What he *really* thinks about on the first date
*His number one excuse for backing out
*How he distinguishes a "good time" from an encounter with lasting *potential*
*What you *never* should do with him the first time out
*His favorite locations for a first kiss
*What it will take to make him make his move

You can win if you know his rules!

Other **Cosmopolitan Books**

THE NICE GIRL'S GUIDE TO SENSATIONAL SEX
THE BEDSIDE ASTROLOGER COMPANION
IRMA KURTZ'S ULTIMATE PROBLEM SOLVER
WHAT MEN WANT FROM THE WOMEN THEY LOVE
ALL THE GOOD MEN ARE *NOT* TAKEN
IS HE THE RIGHT MAN FOR YOU?
STAR SPELLS
WHY DON'T YOU . . .

Coming Soon

WHERE THE BOYS ARE

Cosmopolitan Books are available at special quantity discounts for bulk purchases for sales promotions, premiums, fund raising or educational use. Special books, or book excerpts, can also be created to fit specific needs.

For details write or telephone the office of the Director of Special Markets, Avon Books, Dept. FP, 1350 Avenue of the Americas, New York, New York 10019, 1-800-238-0658.

THE DATING GAME

KEN CARLTON

COSMOPOLITAN

> **VISIT OUR WEBSITE AT**
> http://AvonBooks.com

THE DATING GAME is an original publication of Cosmopolitan Books. This work has never before appeared in book form.

The purpose of this book is to educate and entertain. It is sold with the understanding that the publisher and author are not rendering medical, psychological, or other professional services. The publisher and author shall not be liable or responsible to any person or entity with respect to any loss or damage caused or alleged to be caused directly or indirectly by the information that appears in this book. The names and details of the people whose stories appear in this book have been changed to conceal their identities.

COSMOPOLITAN BOOKS
AVON BOOKS
A division of
The Hearst Corporation
1350 Avenue of the Americas
New York, New York 10019

Copyright © 1996 by Ken Carlton
Published by arrangement with the author
Library of Congress Catalog Card Number: 96-96452
ISBN: 0-380-78799-7

All rights reserved, which includes the right to reproduce this book or portions thereof in any form whatsoever except as provided by the U.S. Copyright Law. For information address Avon Books.

First Cosmopolitan Books Printing: December 1996

COSMOPOLITAN TRADEMARK REG. U.S. PAT. OFF. AND IN OTHER COUNTRIES, MARCA REGISTRADA, HECHO EN U.S.A.

Printed in the U.S.A.

RA 10 9 8 7 6 5 4 3 2 1

> If you purchased this book without a cover, you should be aware that this book is stolen property. It was reported as "unsold and destroyed" to the publisher, and neither the author nor the publisher has received any payment for this "stripped book."

Contents

CHAPTER ONE: WHERE DO THE GUYS HANG OUT? 1
A Kinder, Gentler Pick-up Scene 4
Men at Work 8
Trade Shows and Conventions 14
Boy Places 17
Sign Up! 20
Night Classes 23
Invent Your Own Group 25

CHAPTER TWO: FIRST IMPRESSIONS 28
The Dilemma 32
What Turns a Man On 35
Your Greatest Asset 38
Pulling Away from the Pack at a Party 41
Your Sense of Humor 45
Reality Check 47
The Secret Admirer 50

CHAPTER THREE: THE FIRST DATE 54
Dropping Hints 56
Asking Him Out 58
Grabbing the Check 63
What's on *His* Mind When He Asks *You* Out? 65
The Weekday Dinner Date 69

CONTENTS

The Friday Versus Saturday Night Date	72
The Sunday Date	75
The Office Date	77

CHAPTER FOUR: BLIND DATES: THE AGONY AND THE ECSTASY — **81**
Trust Your Mother, Know Your Friends!	84
Truth in Advertising	89
A Perfect Blind Date	92
The Electronic Date	99
Caution or Passion?	100
A Graceful Exit	103

CHAPTER FIVE: HAVE YOU EVER KISSED A FROG? — **108**
The Shy Guy	113
Can You Date Your Best Friend?	116
"Wounded in Love Seeks Friend in Need . . ."	119
A Mismatch Made in Heaven	123
The Fine Art of Compromise	127
One Last Pitch for the Diamond in the Rough	130

CHAPTER SIX: SEX! — **133**
Mental Foreplay	136
Whose Move Is It Now?	138
The Infinite Possibilities	145
The First Time	148
The Morning After	153
A Few Noteworthy Highlights	157

CHAPTER SEVEN: HOW *NOT* TO BE THE DATE FROM HELL — **161**
First Impressions You Don't Want to Make	164
More First Date Faux Pas	167
Dinner Date Rigor Mortis	170
More of Our Least Favorite Things	174

Sex and the Ex	177
The Dreaded Corner	180
Learning to Laugh	184
CHAPTER EIGHT: FROM DATE TO BOYFRIEND	**188**
If You're Interested, Let Him Know	190
The Dates That Raise the Stakes	193
The Seduction Dance	197
Planning a Lost Weekend	200
The Family Affair	205
Getting Along with the Guys	208
When Is It Time to Share Drawers?	210

ONE

Where Do the Guys Hang Out?

"There are no decent guys out there!" is the lament of countless frustrated, perplexed, and lonely single women.

"I can't find a single decent date!" is the complaint from an equal number of frustrated, perplexed, and lonely single men.

There is probably not a single person in any city, town, or village in this country who hasn't shared these sentiments at some time. Chances are that you have, too.

Still, your friends keep saying that there are tons of handsome, thoughtful, funny, decent, and available single guys out there. Could that be true? Or is it yet another cruel myth perpetuated by the contentedly coupled, who are so settled in their blissful relationships that they've forgotten how hard it was to find a mate? Where are all these eligible men hiding? Can you find one without offering a six-figure dowry or moving to the Alaskan frontier?

* * *

Kitty, a Maine artist, was racing toward her thirtieth birthday without a significant other when she accepted a graphic arts job in Providence, Rhode Island, and left the quiet, little coastal village where she had grown up. Ostensibly this was a career move, but deep down, Kitty hoped that living someplace where there were more than a handful of eligible men would improve her chances of having a meaningful relationship. As month after month went by, though, the big city proved to be no more satisfying in the date department than the small town had been. After a man she had been seeing for three months dumped her to return to his ex, Kitty threw in the towel. She moved back to her seaside hometown, where she wound up learning that there's a great deal of truth to the credo: "Love finds you when you're least looking."

Kitty lived with her parents, painted, took occasional freelance design jobs, and didn't have so much as a single date for half the summer. Then one afternoon, while she was painting down by the marina, a twenty-seven-foot, antique wooden sailboat motored into the harbor and docked. A handsome young man came ashore, bought a sandwich, and made himself comfortable in the warm summer sun on a bench directly behind Kitty and her easel. He sat quietly and watched her work. He observed for so long that she finally turned and asked him what he was so interested in. "Your painting's gotten a lot better since high school, Kitty!" was the guy's reply.

It bewildered Kitty until she recognized Bobby, the former captain of their high school's math team, and realized, much to her surprise, that he *also* had gotten a lot better. A lot better looking. A lot more outgoing. And, as it turned out, a lot more interesting, now that he restored old sailboats for a living. Six months after Kitty and Bobby were reunited on the pier, he proposed to her, and Kitty's fruitless search for a lasting relationship came to an end. She had looked for love in all the wrong places, when it had been right there in her hometown all along.

It would certainly be unrealistic to think that every single woman could return to her hometown and find that the high school nerd had grown up to be the ruggedly handsome, adventurous man of her dreams. By now, our high school classmates are more likely to be long married and driving their kids to Little League in minivans. However, there is a lesson to be learned from Kitty's experience: You don't have to channel incredible amounts of time and energy into your quest for love, or travel far and wide to find a decent guy to date. There's a very good chance that the man you seek is available, searching too, and much closer to home than you might think.

Of course, *meeting* that guy can still be quite a challenge. It may take a lot of luck. But it also takes legwork. If you want to land a decent job, you have to identify openings, fill out applications, and be called in for an interview before you even have a chance to get the position, right? Well, a lot of comparisons can be drawn between job-hunting and finding a satisfying date. Sitting home alone on a Friday night disconsolately watching the Psychic Network or reruns of "Love

Connection," won't improve your odds of meeting a man. What will? The answer is rather obvious: Go where the guys are!

A KINDER, GENTLER PICK-UP SCENE

Let's start our guided tour of male stomping grounds with the most clichéd place to meet someone, and the one people *say* is their least favorite: the bars! Their reputation as notorious pick-up joints is actually rather outdated. In the seventies and early eighties, men and women went to bars to get drunk and lie to one another in the hopes of finding a partner for the night—and more often than not for that night only. But ours was a more promiscuous society then; one in which carefree singles rarely thought twice about having one-night stands.

Today the risk of contracting sexually transmitted diseases, including the deadly AIDS virus (HIV), and a more cautious attitude toward people in general, permeates our culture. Searching for a half-crocked stranger to have sex with is practically unheard of these days. Few intelligent men go to bars for casual pick ups any more, and even fewer women are interested in doing so. Yet the bars themselves continue to thrive, and young, single people of both genders continue to flock to them—albeit with different attitudes.

Bar-hopping is more of a group sport, now, and it's often built around an event or activity (watching the Super Bowl or NCAA tournament, or celebrating someone's birthday). In cities where apartments are too small for a large gathering, bars can be the focal point for single people's social lives. Those that join forces with popular restaurants to offer affordable dining, as well as a relaxed atmosphere for socializing, become the weekend hangout for groups of friends when they don't have formal dates. If you're fairly outgoing and exercise at least as much caution as you would in any other social setting, bars can be ideal places to meet unattached members of the opposite sex.

Neil, a Washington lawyer and exhausted bachelor, discovered this when he met several fellow University of Maryland alumni at a Georgetown bar. Most of the guys brought their wives or girlfriends, and by 10 P.M. the group had grown to about a dozen people, all of them couples, except for Neil. Then one person in his group bumped into another group of former University of Marylanders, most of them women, and "old home week" grew to huge proportions. Neil, who was basically bringing up the rear, soon noticed a very pretty woman who also seemed slightly on the fringe. She smiled shyly at Neil. He smiled back, and immediately made his move. He took advantage of the notion that there's safety in numbers, and told himself that he wasn't really approaching a complete stranger because she was with her friends who knew some of his.

Neil introduced himself and learned that the woman's name was Rachel. She was a Washington attorney, too. Once that basic data was exchanged, it took the two of them all of fifteen seconds to simultaneously utter the mating call of urban singles: *"Don't you just hate hanging out at bars!"* This was their way of saying, "Hey we gotta do this, but if you and I start going out we won't have to do it much longer!" And as it turned out, Rachel and Neil didn't even have to exchange numbers to make a date. A bunch of their now gigantic bar group split off to go to a nearby jazz club. Neil and Rachel joined them, going on their first date straight from the bar, with a half-dozen friends in tow!

Guys go to bars for three reasons: to watch sports, drink beer, and meet women. Consequently, the average male bar-goer wants a venue with lots of unobstructed TV screens, cheap eats, and an attractive female clientele. On a Friday night, he is especially interested in meeting a like-minded woman: someone who wouldn't mind a little lighthearted conversation with a member of the opposite sex while she winds down after a long work week. And he rarely ventures out alone. For instance, Ian, who is rather shy, prefers to hit the Houston bar scene with his best buddy Jeff and a few other guys. Having the guys around guarantees him *some* fun, and it doesn't hurt that Jeff is a drop-dead gorgeous, steely, self-confident woman-magnet.

No matter where they go, Jeff attracts at least one woman's attention, and that woman usually has several friends with her, which gets Ian and the rest of the guys involved in the action too. After Jeff breaks the ice, two groups of people blend into one and sidle up to the bar to party together.

Even if you don't know any *guy* magnets, here's a key piece of advice. Do what Ian does and go to bars in groups. It's safer for you *and* more inviting to men. If you are one-on-one with some *other* guy, we certainly aren't going to come talk to you. It doesn't matter if he's just your brother, how would we know? Likewise, if you're involved in an intense discussion with one female friend, we're not going to interrupt your private conversation and cut in by saying, "Hi. Don't I know you from somewhere?" More likely than not you're going to respond, "No. And I'm talking to a friend, you creep!" Although we can hardly blame you for blowing us off under those circumstances, we still don't enjoy going through the motions.

Men are far more likely to wander over and start up a casual conversation if you are part of a group. Indeed, the sight of four attractive women having a good time together brings out the clown in us, the entertainer, the kid who did handsprings for you when you were ten—and crashed into the hedges because he wasn't watching where he was going. The more of you, the merrier. We're not afraid to make fools of ourselves in front of a crowd. It's seriously asking you out and being seriously rejected that mortifies us. So we'll goof around with a group of you to warm things up, and if no one good-naturedly gives us the boot, we'll begin to direct our attention toward the woman who originally caught our eye, and who could be you.

Navigating the Bar Scene

DO	DON'T
Travel in a pack. Six women watching a game is a male-magnet, and there is safety in numbers. One guy can't become too much of a nuisance if there are six of you!	Go to hotel bars alone on a business trip, unless you are looking to be hit on. But if you must hit the hotel café for a late snack, carry a book! Most guys will get the hint.
Send a guy a beer if he's with a bunch of his friends. It's a great way to get his attention.	Ditch your friends to leave a bar with a man. If he's really interested, he'll make a date with you.
Get his card or office phone number and offer to call him at work.	Give out your home number to a stranger. If he doesn't have a number where he can be reached, you don't want to reach him!

MEN AT WORK

When Noah landed a position as writer on a television sitcom, he quickly learned about an unspoken law on many such shows: The junior staff never goes home before the executive producer. And the executive producer on Noah's show simply never went home. Some staff members weren't even sure he *had* a home! Which meant that Noah and his colleagues put in insane hours crafting episode after episode about the lives of fictitious characters, while their *own* lives ground to a halt.

Being a newcomer to Hollywood, Noah was lucky to be shown the ropes by a pretty young writer's assistant named Joy. She gave him the skinny on all the actors and actresses and clued him in to his bosses' various quirks. Since Noah had virtually no time to establish himself in the Los Angeles area, Joy also helped him find an apartment in a decent neighborhood, a health club, and the best local restaurants. Some of this was done in the spirit of charity. (Joy had seen many an out-of-town writer gobbled up by the system.) But the real fact was Joy had a thing for Noah and she was pursuing him in the age-old tradition of being an exceptionally nice friend.

A joke among Hollywood insiders goes, "Did you hear the one about the dim-witted groupie? She slept with the writer!" Well Joy was neither dim-witted nor a groupie. And Noah, who had never heard this joke, had no reason to suspect that he might be at the bottom of the dating food chain. Through one chaotic, round-the-clock work week after another, they simply grew closer, until they finally crossed the line between work and play. Their first kiss was stolen behind the studio bleachers while a live audience was applauding Noah's first produced episode.

From then on, Joy and Noah pursued their romance on the sly. Neither one of them wanted to see Joy's chances to move up the production company's career ladder jeopardized, or her integrity compromised, because she was sleeping with one of the writers. And they did manage to successfully conduct both their careers and their office romance without affecting the quality of their work (or giving away the creative places they found to make love in a large Hollywood studio). As a result, Joy eventually *was* promoted to assistant producer. Noah later left the show to write and produce another sitcom.

Obviously, Joy and Noah are not the first couple to ever fall in love in the workplace, and they certainly are not the first to keep an entire office from even suspecting that they were having a torrid affair. They both had to use the utmost discretion to pursue a romance that probably would not have been smiled on by their superiors or their colleagues. It is a social art form you too will find useful should you stumble upon a great guy at work.

Finding a date at work is not what it used to be. Today there are a lot more restrictions on both men and women. Some corporations strictly forbid employee dating. And then there is the matter of sexual harassment in the workplace. What was once considered innocent flirtation or joking might now be interpreted as crossing the line of decency. That doesn't mean that dating a workmate is completely out of the question. You simply have to tread more cautiously, select your friends more carefully, and use common sense at all times. If you keep these ground rules in mind and take a good look at the guy in the next cubicle over, you might discover that he has already noticed you.

You see, one of the favorite subjects of men at work are the women in the office they'd like to date (and yes, you can assume by "date" we mean *everything* that entails!). Other than last night's game and our bosses, *you* are the main subjects that dominate our private conversations at the water cooler. The fact of the matter is, an awful lot of men still see the workplace as a veritable playground. We have to be there all day, anyway, and our jobs are not always as interesting as we would like—or at least interesting enough to keep our minds from wandering. Forty to fifty hours a week in the same place, fifty weeks a year, gives us plenty of time to think about the women we work with, and plenty of opportunity to consider asking someone we know fairly well to go out. The question is, how to do that without appearing too obvious or sacrificing the sanctity of our jobs?

In this cautious age of avoiding anything that remotely resembles sexual impropriety, both men and women have to be extremely careful about the way they flirt at work. But the bulk of harassment charges have been leveled at men, and not surprisingly, we have become very reluctant to pick up on signs of interest on your part. We may miss hints that used to seem obvious, because we need to be very sure that we are truly being flirted with by you. And even if we think that is the case, we may not make a move until we have an excuse to take our casual work relationships *out* of the office!

That was the case for Davis, a senior editor at a New Jersey magazine who had his eye on Tina, a young production assistant in the art department. Tina was twenty-four, creative, sexy, happily single and a wiz with the magazine's computerized design program. Davis, on the other hand, was an old-fashioned typewriter guy and truly out of his element when it came to this new technology. He really needed help. Of course, he could have gotten it from any number of designers on the magazine. However, every time he thoroughly screwed up a page, he waited until Tina was the only designer available before seeking help to crawl out of the techno-hole he had buried himself in.

Not only did this only slightly devious ploy allow Davis to spend time with Tina, it also left him clearly and obviously indebted to her for saving his job a half-dozen times. So, one Friday afternoon he asked if he could buy her dinner sometime—to express his gratitude for all the generous help she had given him. There was no pressure involved. If she didn't like him, or didn't feel his gesture was necessary, or didn't think it was appropriate, all she had to say was "no thanks!" But Tina was interested and she agreed to a weeknight drink, which led to a dinner, and then a casual dating relationship.

This is how a guy makes the moves at work today. It's relatively subtle, virtually risk-free flirtation. And working in the same building with the same people on the same projects gives us ample opportunity to test the waters.

What are some creative ways for women to do the same? Get involved in a joint project. Join the office volleyball team. Offer to help him with a computer problem. Ask if he needs someone to proofread a report he is working on. Or solicit *his* assistance. Ask his advice on a difficult assignment. Query him about the best approach to take with a superior. Have him kick the soda machine for you after you've lost your four-thousandth quarter in it!

No one needs to know that you have more than a passing interest in the guy down the hall. Working together on some aspect of a project simply opens the door for you to get to know one another a little better. If there's mutual interest, you can take it outside the office. And if there isn't, you both have an easy out.

When you ask a man for advice on a project, he can jump at the opportunity to help. Or he can beg off because he's too busy. Maybe he truly is. And even if he does suspect that you are flirting with him, he is not necessarily rejecting you personally. He is simply making a business decision, the same kind you make every day.

Perhaps the nicest thing about working with members of the opposite sex is that we can get to know each other without so much as a whisper of a date. When you land on a project with a man whom you may or may not have had your eye on, you can discover all sorts of interesting things about him. Through casual conversation, you might learn that he had his heart dashed to pieces by his last lover and is in no shape to date. Or you might find out that the quiet guy with glasses has a thing for bondage and cross-dressing, which may or may not be your thing, too. People make strange remarks when they're working under pressure at three in the morning. That little office flirtation might spare you the disappointment of a future failed date.

On the other hand, you could discover that you and your fellow account manager both love obscure art films, and you can conveniently mention the Polish film festival that just happens to be playing at the local cinema. It's the perfect excuse to make a date without officially calling it a date—although you both know it is. You can go out under the guise of sharing a mutual interest, and at the very least gain valuable insight into Polish culture. Or you could land in a terrific, not entirely unexpected romance.

Office Opening Salvos

WHEN HE SAYS:	WHAT IT MEANS:
"Do you know anything about the 401K seminar this afternoon?"	*If you're going, I'm going! Anything that puts us in the same room.*
"Do you need help with that copy machine jam?"	*Wanna look under the hood of my vintage Mustang this weekend?*
"I didn't know Smith and McBride are dating?"	*If they can get away with it, so can we. Are you free tonight?*

TRADE SHOWS AND CONVENTIONS

If you've never been to a trade show or professional convention, it's time to find out what you're missing. They are typically staged in a popular tourist city—San Francisco or New Orleans or Las Vegas or Miami, to name a few. At a large hotel or convention center, hundreds, and sometimes a thousand or more companies set up booths to display their wares. During the day, sales executives and support staff, many of whom have been on the trade-show circuit for years, work their booths and the floor, often catching up with business acquaintances as if they were meeting at a college reunion. The night is reserved for cocktails and business dinners, and in the glitzier fields, large theme parties to roll out new products. While trade shows can be hard work, they often have the feel of one big business party.

At one such show in Las Vegas, Dan, a mid-level executive at a Connecticut digital technology firm, met Carol, who represented a London company that occasionally did business with Dan's. The first spark of attraction occurred in a casino on the Vegas strip where they sat until dawn playing five-dollar blackjack and, believe it or not, talking shop. (People who work trade shows often conduct business in some very unusual situations.) Transatlantic faxes kept their business friendship going until they both attended another trade show three months later in Singapore.

They flew halfway around the world to hawk computer wares, stayed in the same fancy hotel, and along with eight or ten other conventioneers, usually got together for dinner at the end of each day to relax from the hectic work schedule. At that point, Carol and Dan had been together socially at four or five business functions, and even shared a business breakfast together several times without either one even bringing up the notion of dating. Yet the attraction was unmistakable.

After Singapore the faxes continued, and Dan found himself looking for an excuse to see Carol again. He found it when another convention was scheduled for Cannes in the south of France. Dan and Carol both turned up there, but on this particular trip, schedule conflicts kept them apart for most of the week. With his trip coming to an end and their friendship established, Dan felt it was safe to ask Carol out, and did exactly that on the last night of the show.

The French Riviera is a marvelous place to conduct business and an even better spot for romance. Dan and Carol escaped the hordes of conventioneers and journeyed a few miles away to a quaint French village for a leisurely country dinner. They discussed France and French food and wines. They talked about each others' lives, loves, and passions. Everything except business. At dawn, overlooking Cannes Harbor, Dan kissed Carol goodnight and then went straight to the airport. A day later, when they returned to their respective home offices, they discovered they had simultaneously sent each other large bouquets of flowers. Call that a very good sign! At last count, Dan and Carol were still involved in a delightful long distance relationship.

The convention and trade show scene can be an excellent meeting ground for young single professionals. It allows you to see fellow employees in a new light outside of the office. And if you're leery about dating someone from your own company, there are droves of other people in your field to choose from, including many you've previously connected with by phone, fax and e-mail. Conventions aren't intended to be meat markets. People are there to do business. But there *are* countless luncheons and dinners and cocktail parties where you can casually socialize, make professional contacts, *and* if you happen to hit it off with someone you like, develop a more personal relationship.

Fields that Offer Great Conventions and Travel Opportunities

- Television
- Film
- Travel
- Publishing
- Public Relations
- Computers
- Electronics
- Food and Hotel Services
- New Technologies

BOY PLACES

Denver natives Gail and Jo were suffering through a serious male drought in their social lives when they decided to check out the local bowling palace. They weren't avid bowlers by any stretch of the imagination. They simply had heard that a certain bowling alley was supposed to be really fun and packed with people on a Saturday night. They dressed down and took to the alley, where they learned there was an hour wait for a lane. A bit of good fortune, as it turned out. Within ten minutes of putting down their names and settling in for the wait, Gail and Jo had met four guys who were positively thrilled to see two nice women just hanging out and waiting to bowl a few games. A friendly conversation ensued and their Saturday night foray turned into a large, casual group date.

Plenty of men don't have dates on a Saturday night, but it is not our style to spend the evening at home. On the other hand, it's not likely you'll find a bunch of lonely guys lining up for the city ballet, or catching a benefit at the local art museum. The fact is, single men often flock to boy places; locations where guys can act like guys. By claiming these places as our own, we aren't waving "sexist" banners. Most of these places aren't filled with men because women are turned away at the door. Nine times out of ten, we'd welcome your company. We'd be thrilled to run into a group of like-minded women on what's traditionally been our turf. Consider these places if you think you'd feel comfortable hanging out with guys on a very casual basis.

Baseball parks are a great bet. What's more fun than a huge group hanging out in the sunshine cheering on the home team. So call your pals and go! We love it when you show up with your friends at the game. Baseball tickets are more readily available than those for most other sports, and reasonably priced. Of course, you may not find yourselves sitting next to an award-winning playwright or the lead singer from your favorite band. But I can virtually guarantee that on a warm weekend afternoon, the ballpark will be filled with lots of fun-minded guys with whom you could have a great time.

Try the tennis courts! Tennis is a great coed sport and very conducive to mixed doubles. So dust off your racket, head down to the local courts with a girlfriend, and scope things out while you wait to play. If you aren't asked to be part of a doubles match the first time out, play singles every weekend for a month. Get to know the familiar faces on the court. Then invite players of similar ability to join you for a future doubles match.

The same notion applies to the golf driving range. Granted, driving golf balls begins as something of a solo sport, but there isn't a guy who's ever wrapped his hands around a club who won't offer to help a novice with her swing. And that works two ways. If you and your girlfriend are driving out a few buckets of balls and you notice a guy who looks like he's trying to beat out a grass fire with his five-iron, offer your kindly assistance. How many friendly lessons away from an afternoon on the local golf course might that be?

As you've probably noticed by now, most of the traditional places men hang out are somehow related to sports. You're just not going to meet hordes of guys at a country antique show or a quilt-making exhibition—although you might meet the occasional male quilter or serious antique lover. Realistically though, most men are more likely to be doing something physical or competitive (or watching other guys do something physical or competitive). So, any activity you and your girlfriends can think of that men seem to like to do together on a weekend afternoon is an activity you should consider doing, too.

Go to the park. Bring a football, a Frisbee, your

dog and a picnic basket. Parks are a great coed playground for single people. Throw on your shorts and sneakers, grab your bicycle, and put yourself into play. We'll be out there, tossing a ball or playing soccer or just hanging out. And you'll never run into a group of us who wouldn't be delighted to have our day brightened by a group of you looking to have a good time, too.

SIGN UP!

I hate to say it, but your mother, grandmother and Great-aunt Matilda were right. You can meet men and have fun times in general if you get involved with groups that draw together people with similar interests.

If you like hiking, join the Sierra Club (or similarly nature-minded organizations). You'll get out of your apartment and into the great outdoors. Plus most of us would agree: A little exercise never hurt anyone. Join a jogging or cycling club and you're going to meet people who exercise at your own pace. You can fall in love training to break the marathon record, *or* hang at the back of the pack and get to know people who like to move at your speed.

If you've always wanted to become more active in your community, join a volunteer organization. They always need able bodies. Check with your church. Contact existing programs, from Big Brothers and Sisters to the local soup kitchen. Or organize a group from your office to clean run-down neighborhoods or repair school classrooms. Not only will you meet people who share in your civic-mindedness, but you'll be pitching in to better the city you live in.

Have you been a sideline athlete since your college days but would like to get back on a team? Try signing up for your office or community softball league. Coed leagues attract lots of singles and thrive on good-natured enthusiasm as much as talent. If you can't swing a bat and wouldn't know a cut-off man from your electricity meter reader, a half-dozen overly eager guys will be delighted to help you learn. Besides, on a team of fifteen, at least seven (both men *and* women) are totally inept, which guarantees that you won't embarrass yourself any more than the next guy. For some reason, softball games often spawn picnics, barbecues, and large, boisterous groups of spectators. And, if you still aren't sold, consider this. There's something in our genetic makeup that causes guys to flip over women in sweatshirts, shorts and ballcaps. You could be tripping over third base or dropping every ball that comes to you, but as long as you're wearing your ballcap, we'll adore you. Go figure!

Then there are singles groups. Now don't skip this page immediately. Somewhere between the horrific thought of glittering disco globes hovering over half-empty ballrooms, or a bunch of beefy guys in thong bikinis playing volleyball on an unknown island beach, singles groups have evolved. These days they tend to form around specific interests, and as a result, even though meeting someone of the opposite sex may still be most group members' goal, they also get to enjoy other activities.

Singles groups affiliated with various religions are very common. For example, Simchat Torah, the Jewish holiday celebrating the reading of the torah, is traditionally a very festive occasion. And on New York City's Upper West Side, it's cause for one of the greatest singles gatherings you'll ever see. Jewish men and women gather from all over the United States and the world to congregate and celebrate and meet members of the opposite sex. When the weather is nice, the festivities have been known to spill out onto the streets and grow into one huge block party.

The value of joining a singles group organized around your religion is that you're sure to be with people who share at least one common value with you. While that is no guarantee of "a love connection," for people who feel strongly about dating within their faith this is obviously a good leaping-off place.

Other singles groups evolve out of activities ranging from ballroom dancing to charity fund-raising. While some are explicitly singles-oriented, others are a bit more understated. At a singles dance or in a group that encourages singles membership, you are thrown into a situation where everyone has the same goal on their mind. Participants generally have a willing and positive attitude about meeting people at these events, but give you a chance to check out the field before making your move. Should you happen upon someone who catches your eye or wins your attention, it's a very short leap from chatting by the punch bowl to trading phone numbers for a future date.

Night Classes

Plenty of people enroll in night classes primarily to meet other people. You can choose something as obvious as dance class, which pairs up men and women during the lessons and attracts a high number of single people looking to meet. If your heart is in it, dance classes can be ripe with opportunity. But for some, this might feel too much like a forced date with a complete stranger and as a result, very uncomfortable. If the very thought makes you squirm, you should look elsewhere in the course catalogue.

Theoretically, taking courses typically populated by members of the opposite sex, auto repair, for example, should provide a vast new dating pool to wade in. But signing up with this notion in mind can backfire as Scot and Michael, two work buddies from the Seattle area, discovered. Utterly sick of their bad luck in the dating scene, they decided to take a class for no other reason than to meet women. And needlepoint seemed the perfect choice—*until* they arrived at the adult education campus, walked into the assigned classroom and discovered that ten other similarly minded men and *no* women had signed up!

There are countless other adult education choices that are low on meat-market potential, but still offer the possibility of meeting someone who shares a similar interest with you. Your best bet is to ask yourself what you've always wanted to learn and then study your local newspaper or city magazine to find where those programs are offered.

How about photography, writing, or cooking

classes? Almost everyone can use generic skills like these. You could develop knowledge or a hobby that will benefit you, even if you don't meet a terrific guy!

Take Maddie, a computer programmer who worked in a high tech office completely populated by men with pencil packs in their shirt pockets. Work just wasn't providing her with many dating opportunities. So Maddie, who had a secret passion for cooking, signed up for a six-week, Saturday morning "Learn-to-cater-as-a-business" class. "Just for the fun of it," she said, although she wasn't about to complain if she met a wonderful guy there. And within an hour of the first class, she did.

John and Maddie hit it off instantly. They chopped, stirred, sautéed, diced, and laughed up a storm, but had absolutely no romantic interest in one another. They maintained their friendship after classes ended, though, and when John's catering business began to take off, he convinced Maddie to leave her job and join forces with him. Six months after their first meeting, John and Maddie were running a small but successful catering company. Maddie loved her new job. Being good at it boosted her self-esteem, which paved the way for her to make new friends and develop a rich new dating life.

Classes Boys Enjoy

- Photography
- French Cooking
- Wine Tasting
- Fiction Writing
- Standup Comedy/Acting
- Refinishing Furniture
- Starting Your Own Business

INVENT YOUR OWN GROUP

Hank, a bachelor and an extraordinarily bored insurance adjuster from Oregon, had sky-high aspirations: He wanted to jump out of a plane. Not because his social life was *that* bad, and definitely not without a parachute. He had simply gotten hooked on the idea after reading an article about first-time skydiving. In time, Hank found a certified school that gave day-long classes, which he could either sign up for as an individual or take with a group of ten to get a good discount rate. He chose the latter and not only managed to live out a lifelong dream, but also pulled together an exciting bunch of young, single men and women who shared an interest in death-defying feats. When last heard from, they were planning a bungee-jumping trip to Colorado!

We all occasionally wallow in self-pity over the desperate straits of trying to find a date for the weekend. It's very easy to belly up to the bar with the guys, or camp out in front of the TV for a long weekend of lamenting our single status. Fortunately, it only takes one or two innovative people to round up a group and turn the dull rut of datelessness into a busy calendar of planned events.

Are you of the literary bent? Start a book group. Get on your office computer and find six friends who like to read. Call your best guy friend and tell him to do the same. Make an effort to include a number of work friends or acquaintances who don't know each other well. Then pick a book, give everyone a few weeks to read it, and meet at your favorite literary bar or restaurant to have a book party. If you get a solid group going it can become a monthly dinner party at someone's home. Whenever someone drops out or can't handle a new novel that month, encourage someone in the group to find a new friend to sit in.

Do you have acquaintances who consider themselves theater buffs? Then group tickets are the way to go. Again, turn to several friends in different walks of life and generate interest from fifteen or twenty people. What nicer way to have a theater date than with a whole new group of people who you can also meet afterwards for a big, family-style dinner? You don't have to advertise your theater night as a singles event. That might be off-putting to some. But single men and women who want to connect with people of like interests know the score. And there is something about an intellectual pursuit that feels a little less threatening. At the very least you'll see the latest show. And more likely than not, new friendships will be forged, another play selected, and you'll have the beginning of your own private club.

In the summertime, many major cities have outdoor concert series in large parks. New York's Central Park can draw one-hundred thousand people to a popular performance. To go it alone may seem about as desirable as being trapped on the subway during a heat wave. But a couple of friends can organize the outing, stake out a good blanket spot on the lawn and tell everyone to bring salads and cheeses and breads and wine. You can have a terrific time that evening plus start a tradition for a devoted group of music lovers.

The variety of ways to draw singles together in a non-threatening manner is almost limitless. Will guys actually respond to some of these suggestions? You bet. If we give the impression that we're not social animals on occasion, it's probably because we're lousy planners. We need a little push. We honestly don't want to spend the rest of our adult lives in dark bars watching basketball with each other. We'd like to be out on dates. But we have trouble meeting women as much as you have trouble meeting us. This means we're all caught in the same predicament, looking for a reason, *any* reason, to get together. We're open to finding new places to hang out and have a good time, mainly because we know we have to get out the front door if there is any hope of meeting that special someone who catches our eye!

TWO

First Impressions

Saturday night. Hermosa Beach, California. Barry, a 25-year-old advertising executive and a half-dozen of his friends are drinking beer and listening to a local band at a popular beach hangout. The place is teeming with single women, but Barry keeps company with three couples and his lonesome. Why? Because he is still suffering the ravages of an especially painful heartbreak.

Nearly a year ago his college sweetheart, the love of his life, had leapt at a job opportunity in San Francisco. A long-distance affair followed, but was abruptly terminated when Barry surprised his girlfriend with a midweek visit and she surprised him with a new boyfriend. Devastated, Barry wallowed in singlehood for almost a year—which is not to say he never went out. He dated around. His sex life thrived. His credit card bills soared. Occasionally a good time was had by all. But not one of the women involved moved Barry the way his old girlfriend had. The chemistry just wasn't there!

This Saturday night is different though. While

his friends frolic on the dance floor and he sits by himself warming a barstool, something happens to Barry. A woman sitting alone at the other end of the bar catches his eye. She wears faded jeans, a white T-shirt, and her brown hair pulled back in a simple ponytail. She is not the most stunning woman in the place. Her body wasn't lifted from the pages of *Playboy*. As a matter of fact, at first glance there is nothing exceptional about her. Yet, for one second, amidst the gyrating bodies, smoke, and noise of the packed bar, Barry notices this woman, and this woman notices him.

She smiles, and Barry does a serious double take. While he sits there opening and closing his mouth like a flounder, the woman gives him another cute grin, laughs, and turns away. Then the band goes on break. The woman's friends crowd back around her. And Barry's friends rejoin him at the bar, blocking his view—though not before the electric bolt that just shot through him nearly knocks him off his barstool!

This is it. The moment every man waits for. It may not happen in a bar or with a total stranger, but the instant it does happen, he knows! *Knows what,* you ask? He *knows* that something amazing has just occurred. He *knows* that if he could just meet you all would be well in the world. Your first date would be one long comfortable glow of conversation and laughter. Your first kiss would be perfect, your first lovemaking warm and the first weekend together blissful. He also *knows* that he must find a way to ask you out, even if he has to use every last ounce of nerve to do it.

Twenty minutes later, Barry still has not mustered up the courage to make his move, and time is running out. As his friends get ready to leave, he casts his thousandth glance in the woman's direction. However, she is deep in conversation with not one, but two hunky guys and has not made eye contact again. With his buddy tugging on his sleeve, Barry fabricates a reason to stay for a few more minutes, and excuses himself.

Barry fights for the barman's attention, points out the woman at the end of the bar, and orders her a drink. Not a beer. Not a margarita. Not a glass of wine. But a strawberry milk! That's right, a strawberry milk. For reasons that will forever remain a mystery, Barry insists that the barman pour a glass of milk, add a dash of strawberry-flavored liqueur, and deliver the concoction to the mystery woman, courtesy of the nice guy at the corner of the bar.

Perched on his barstool, Barry watches as the bartender hands the woman the glass of strawberry milk. When she leans forward and, yelling to be heard, asks who sent the drink, he points in Barry's direction. She searches the crowded bar until her eye catches his. She points at the drink and then at herself and raises an eyebrow as if to ask, "Why me?" In response, Barry walks over and introduces himself. "You just looked as if you could use a glass of strawberry milk from a nice guy at a crowded bar on a Saturday night!" he explains.

Well, the recipient of Barry's admittedly odd gesture could have laughed in his face. Or ignored him. Or dumped the strawberry milk in his lap and told him to try his weird moves on someone else. But luck, fate, the stars, or *something* is in

Barry's favor on this particular eve because the woman, whose name is Joni, is amused. And after talking to Barry for a few minutes, she is charmed. And after four months of dating, she is taken enough to accept his engagement ring (presented to her at an elegant restaurant in an ice bucket with a glass of strawberry milk)!

Here is a proposition for you. Open your eyes and look around. Take note of three men you've never noticed before. Skip Quasimodo, Lurch and the office lech from the sixth floor. Don't set your sights on the company stud, the Olympic jock and the married senior vice president either. None of them are available! Instead, pay attention to a friend at work or a student in your acting class or the okay guy you ride the elevator with every morning.

Why am I asking you to do this? Because I know that somewhere in your life—at work or school, at church or the grocery store or your health club— there is a nice guy you already know whom you'd probably find attractive if you gave him half a chance. He's got a real job and a real life. There's nothing wrong with him and he isn't dating anyone. He's definitely aware of you. Okay, he's probably not losing sleep or reciting your name like a mantra, yet. But he's out there and he's noticed that you have a pretty smile or a nice figure or a way about you that he finds appealing.

So, why hasn't he asked you out? Most likely because he doesn't know how. Maybe you've never said hello to him. Maybe you don't even know he's there. And he doesn't want to impose. Maybe he's a little shy or scared of rejection. Perhaps, like Barry, he's been burned recently and worries about getting hurt again. Which makes you wonder: Could it be that the problem preventing you from meeting that special someone is *not* a lack of potential dates but rather a lack of communication? Or access? Or nerve?

THE DILEMMA

There are two kinds of single men. The first kind thrive on playing the field. They go on date after date after date, often (or at least as often as they can) sleeping with that evening's companion. You women have coined a term for such men. You call them *pigs!*

Of course, there are plenty of women who enjoy playing the field just as much as guys do—which is why easy guys pretty regularly meet willing women and they both get a little nookie on a Saturday night. Nine times out of ten, they wake up together on a Sunday morning and wonder what the heck they're doing in bed with a complete stranger. Maybe they go through the motions and pretend to like one another. More often than not though, they mumble their farewells, scurry into the bright sunlight and toss a hastily scribbled phone number into the nearest trash can. As games go, this one is fairly harmless so long as both players know what they're getting into (and play it safely). But that's only one definition of dating.

There are also countless men with an entirely different take on the situation. Getting you into bed is *not* the first thing on their minds. These guys might fantasize about eventually having sex with you, but they are drawn to you for other reasons. They'd like to invite you over for a nice romantic dinner. Or spend a relaxing weekend hanging out in the park, visiting a museum or going to a Sunday afternoon movie. They're willing to jump through a few hoops and manufacture a big-deal date or two for your benefit—even though they'd probably prefer something more casual. Men love it when a woman they feel something special for is happy just being around them.

Sure, men like the chase. And we have no problem with an occasional unfettered leap into the sack. But the mature man—the one with his eye on the future—doesn't really like being unattached. He longs to meet a woman, ask her out, have a couple of nice, let's-get-acquainted dates with her, and eventually see his efforts blossom into a meaningful, lasting relationship.

Of course, before any man can set out on this romantic mission, one tiny little event has to occur. He has to be where you are and notice you and be attracted to you. In terms that go way beyond science or medicine, there has to be a spark, an inexplicably, utterly intoxicating initial connection, a first impression that leaves him yearning to know you better—and for more than one night. There are countless examples of how men perceive that initial spark, some more romantic than others.

For example, in Manhattan's trendy SoHo district, a cocky young man named Steve stopped into a coffee bar densely populated by the denizens of New York's fashion scene and almost immediately spotted a woman who made his pulse race. She wasn't a tall, leggy model or famous face. What drew Steve to her was the sheer, see-through blouse she was wearing with *nothing* underneath. Steve, a great preacher of truth in relationships, walked up to her, introduced himself and commented on how lovely he found her breasts. Believe me, he was speaking the mind of every guy in the place. Unfortunately for Steve, she was clearly offended by what he said—or maybe it was the fact that he couldn't tear his gaze away from her chest. Either way, she responded by calmly pouring her iced cappuccino down his pants.

Although you may cheer this move as a symbolic victory for every woman who has ever been leered at by a lecherous man, the fact remains that baring your breasts (or anything else so provocative) almost always guarantees you a panting, howling audience of hound dogs whenever you go out and wherever you go. It doesn't do you much good if your aim is to attract a nice guy to date, though. (Would *you* go out with a man who came to a concert or cocktail party wearing a tight pair of dolphin shorts and no underwear? I doubt it, otherwise lots of guys would probably dress that way!)

To ignite a nice guy's interest, you don't need see-through blouses or breast implants, dyed hair, oceanic green contact lenses, or a thousand-dollar outfit. You can bear absolutely no resemblance to Claudia Schiffer, Sharon Stone or Cindy Crawford, and still knock us out. While it's true that men *are* visually oriented, that doesn't mean we only respond to the obvious. Looks are *not* the only thing we go for. In fact, I'll go out on a limb here and suggest that looks are relatively unimportant—once you've caught a man's eye. While the initial spark that ignites his interest *is* based on your physical appearance to some extent, it is also momentary, fleeting and for the most part, a coincidence rather than the result of anything you can calculate or control.

Yes, if you pile on the makeup or shave your head and go to a party dressed in Saran Wrap, that might turn a man's head. It would probably turn quite a few heads. But the guy you're longing to meet—the one you've had your eye on for three months—will only be captivated if there is something about the way you look that taps into his *heart*.

Just ask Rick, a fitness trainer at a trendy Chicago health club who spends six days a week coaxing the trim bodies of the Windy City's finest into even better shape. He has seen more than his fair share of women, most of them in a sweaty, semi-dressed state. And he has had ample opportunity to date any number of these perfect tens. Yet, his longtime lover is an office manager in her mid-thirties, who dresses conservatively and has a slightly better than average figure, but nothing near the sculpted hardbodies Rick works on every day.

What Turns a Man On

There is no way to predict or control what will make a particular man's head spin. In the looks department alone, you can ask a thousand guys what turns them on and get two thousand different answers. The list of what we find physically attractive could go on for pages. Our preferences simply are not as narrowly defined as women sometimes like to think.

One of the biggest misconceptions women have about men is that we all like large breasts. Not true! For every man who falls for a woman of prodigious proportions, there is another who is totally turned on by the slight-chested. Likewise, the six-foot model type is *not* every man's first choice. Just as many of us will stop in our tracks for a five-foot-two lab technician with her hair pinned back and wire-rimmed glasses perched on her nose. And *not all men* like blonde hair, blue eyes, long legs, skinny butts, or pouty lips.

Our taste isn't one-size-fits-all when it comes to clothes, either. Should you wear tight, short skirts? Thong bikinis? Lacy lingerie? Sure, some guys flip for the blatantly sexy. But every guy defines "sexy" differently, and plenty of us are drawn to "subtle and understated." Cozy sweatshirts and well-worn jeans can make us stumble over our words just as much as handsome suits and flowing dresses can be turn-ons too.

This concept really isn't that difficult to grasp. After all, are you only attracted to tall, dark-haired, brown-eyed hunks, and no one else will do? Or could you also find yourself warming up to a perfectly ordinary, pleasant-looking man with a great sense of humor? When faced with the reality of finding a mate we find attractive, we all could stand to be as open-minded as possible.

Men may be oglers and gazers and voyeurs. But most of us simply are not seeking some media definition of the perfect woman. As a matter of fact, if you're walking down a crowded street during a springtime lunch hour, there is sure to be at least one nice guy who finds *you* attractive, regardless of what you look like. Seeing you is going to do such a number on him that he'll narrowly miss getting hit by a cab or nearly bowl over an old lady just trying to get another glimpse. He's going to think about you for the rest of the day. He'll wonder if you hang out at the same café every afternoon. He'll start conjuring up ways to bump into you again. And he'll do all this because he's attracted to the unique, quirky combination of qualities that make you who you are, and all the trendy clothes or plastic surgery in the world can't and shouldn't change that.

Top 10 Turn-ons for Most Men

1. Breasts (*all* shapes, *all* sizes)
2. Butts (ditto)
3. Great Smile
4. Striking Hair
5. Pretty Eyes
6. Muscular calves
7. Thighs
8. Short Skirts
9. Aggressive Personality
10. High Heels

Your Greatest Asset

Mark, a freelance computer web site designer, was invited to a country club get-together hosted by a client and populated mainly by conservative financial types. Being a happy-go-lucky, starving-artist type himself, Mark did his best to fit in, but found he had little in common with the few people he managed to meet. He exhausted his supply of cutting-edge business conversation within an hour and retreated outside for one last beer and a cigarette before heading home. As he surveyed the action on the patio, he felt a tap on his shoulder and spun around to face an attractive woman dressed all in black. She asked him if he could spare a smoke. Mark was taken aback, first, because he had not expected to find anyone else at this corporate gathering who would be caught dead smoking, and second, because this very alluring woman had somehow escaped his eye during the course of the evening.

Mark was more than happy to hand over a cigarette to the woman in black (whose name was Julie), and he sat there slack-jawed, admiring her, as she assertively commandeered the bartender and ordered a bone-dry martini straight up with two olives. Finally, he offered her a light. She accepted, placing the cigarette between her lips, cupping Mark's match hand with *both* of hers, and applying the slightest gentle pressure as he held the match. Talk about sexy. The connection was tangible. Suddenly the party had new life.

Mark and Julie started talking. She turned out to be a stage manager for a small theater. He happened to know an actor in her current production. Somehow the only two artist types in a roomful of bankers had found each other. The conversation flowed. They had another drink and shortly decided to leave the "boardroom" for a more funky lounge. Not surprisingly, they ended up dating.

Although he won't deny the appeal of her unusual looks or svelte body, what Mark remembers most about their initial meeting was Julie's boldness and the fact that she, like Mark, didn't really fit in at the party. While she didn't wildly boast about it, he could tell how creative she was, and this also attracted him. Her own distinctive personality drew him in.

Okay, so you've noticed him. He's noticed you. You've both noticed a spark, an electric current sizzling between you. A subconscious decision is made to go down a new road together. To talk. Flirt. Maybe more. You can't manufacture this sort of attraction. You can't plan or design or buy it. "IT" just happens. When you both realize "something's going on here," *then* your personality becomes everything.

If the man in question is looking to you only for a sexual liaison, your personality will be the last thing on his mind. You can usually tell this quickly. If his wild-eyed, panting leer doesn't give him away, his opening salvo or first few minutes of cliché-filled conversation generally will. (Does anyone really buy those silly "come on" lines any more?) Likewise, if you're looking at *him* just for a quick romp on the sofa, then you're probably as unconcerned with his personality as he is with yours. But if you and he have "connected" and are ready to pursue the attraction further, it's your personality that will convince him to continue.

Regardless of where a man's eyes may wander (he can't help but scope out your body; it's a natural reflex), after he strikes up that first conversation with you, you can bet he's desperately hoping you're a winner, not just physically, but in every sense of the word. And since he can't learn everything about you in two minutes, he'll key in on any telltale facet of your character that grabs his interest and makes him want to know more.

If you subscribe to the symphony and a man sees you by yourself at intermission every Sunday, he's going to remember you. Not just for your pretty smile, but because of the statement you're making: You like classical music enough to go to the concerts alone. That is a bold and sexy character trait that will make an awe-inspiring first impression every time.

Men are attracted to as many different personalities as they are to different looks. They are turned on by the athletic, homespun girl-next-door as well as the dark, mysterious woman who spends Sunday afternoons in museums analyzing modern art. We like driven, corporate go-getters and devoted arts-and-crafts types; demonstrative, stand-up comediennes and shy, soft-spoken bookworms. We can't imagine the personality type that some man isn't going to be drawn to. But don't go trying to *become* someone you're not! It's not fair for us to expect you to, and it's not possible—for women *or* men. We all search for people who will be attracted to who we *really* are.

Pulling Away from the Pack at a Party

Throw two hundred strangers in a room. Fill it with loud music and smoke and drunken bodies and dancing. Can you imagine a more difficult place to try to meet someone?

How do you get noticed at a packed party or a mobbed bar? What do you do when you're a five-foot-two brunette in a roomful of six-foot-two blondes? How do you stand out from the rest of the crowd?

Men at parties lump women into two groups: standoffish or approachable. Any man can spot the former type of woman from a mile away. She surrounds herself with several standoffish friends and seems to critique every male who walks into the room. If one is lucky enough to make eye contact with her, it doesn't last for more than an instant before she turns her head and titters as if she's just noticed he has a stump of celery protruding from between his front teeth. She rebuffs every offer of kindness and effort to get to know her. "Can I get you a drink?" "Have you tried the bruschetta?" "Didn't we meet at the opera last year?" All queries receive the same response. "No, no, and absolutely not!"

"Unfair," you say. "Why should this woman have to make small talk with every stranger who crosses her path?" Well, she doesn't *have* to. She is free to set herself off from the crowd and only speak with the people she knows intimately and shoo the rest of us off like horseflies at the beach. That's her prerogative. But being a snob is not going to win her many friends. Most guys would agree that a woman who comes off as a snob at a party is a woman they'd just as soon not meet. In fact, they're likely to run, not walk to the opposite side of the room when they feel the first chill of her icy attitude. Warming up this woman is hard work and a lot of men prefer not to work that hard to meet a woman at a party. The one possible exception is a guy who'll make a play for her because he's into conquests. As in, "I bet I can get the ice queen into bed!"

On the opposite end of the spectrum is someone like Liza, a secretary by day and struggling actress by night who is the epitome of approachability. Perhaps wearing so many hats in her professional life has made her more adaptable than most. Maybe acting has taught her to open herself up to many different situations. Or it could be that having a second career that intrigues people means she always has something to talk about. But whatever the explanation, when Liza attends corporate functions, she is the hit of the evening.

She is constantly surrounded by men. Driven, twenty-hour-work-day executives appreciate the panache she brings to what might otherwise be a duller affair. Similarly, in the theater world, Liza relies on her experiences in the "real" world to keep her on an even keel. She is as comfortable chatting with a fellow actor as she is discussing financing with a would-be producer. Wherever Liza goes, she brings an open mind and an honest interest in the various people she meets.

A party is a social gathering and whether men are looking for a date, a one-night stand, or a business contact, they tend to approach parties as Liza does—with a totally open mind. We are primed to meet women. We're "in the mood." And as you've probably noticed, we are mostly devoid of shame. We accept the fact that we might make fools of ourselves, and then we plow into uncharted waters in the hopes we can minimize the damage, if not actually make a good first impression.

The same can be said for the "approachable" woman. An open mind is a provocative conversation starter. What other qualities define the woman guys want to meet? A sense of humor. A spirit of adventure. A bit of good-natured self-deprecation. A warm smile. A firm handshake. And the chutzpah to say to a man, *"Hey, who are you? Wanna dance?"*

This doesn't mean that you have to welcome every man in the place with open arms and give him an hour of your time. But if you've made the effort to get dressed up and go to a party, it can't hurt to give the guys there a chance. Make small talk. Laugh at a few bad jokes. Pawn off the oddballs on the strange woman you just met ten minutes ago. ("Say Bill, that's really interesting about your pet iguana. See that woman over there with the dark hair—she just was telling me how much she loves reptiles. You should go introduce yourself!")

Don't instantly write off a man just because he isn't quite what you were looking for. For one thing, you wouldn't want men to be that harsh with you. And besides, he might have cute friends. After all, performance artists have been known to share apartments with investment bankers! And maybe this party *is* a dud. But how do you know you won't bump into that guy with the shaved head and sunglasses next week at another party, where he'll be hanging out with the man of your dreams? If that happens, won't you be infinitely glad that you took the five minutes to chat with him the first time you met?

So accept a party for what it is: an opportunity to meet a lot of different people and do a bit of self-promotion. It's free advertising, and the product is *you*. Flaunt your best personality traits. Tell a funny story. Tap dance. Hand out a picture of your dog. Sing a song. Men will respond. Sure, some will run. But others will join in and strike up the chorus in perfect harmony with you. At the very least, a guy who loves the picture of your dog will be looking for a partner to jog with him and his beagle in the park on Saturday mornings.

Memorable Eye-Opening Lines
Said by Women
(As reported by the guys who heard them)

"I'm having trouble getting the top down on my convertible. Would you mind giving me a hand with my *Mercedes?*"

—Chaz, a Dallas doctor

"I love walking in the rain. Say, do you want to blow this party and get wet with me?"

—Rick, an Atlanta salesman

"I'm sorry to bother you. Can you do me a favor and help me make my ex-boyfriend over there really jealous?"

—Jack, a Detroit truck driver

Your Sense of Humor

For their entire dating lives, men have been hearing that the number one thing women are looking for in a man is a sense of humor. A lot of men tend to be a bit skeptical about this theory, possibly because we've seen so many terrific women going out with really humorless guys who drive Porsches. (No one ever said life is fair.) We'll agree however—laughter is good. Men definitely place a "sense of humor" high on the list of traits we look for in a woman. In fact, we need you to have a sense of humor because we do some incredibly foolish things while we're working up the nerve to ask you out on a first date.

A lawyer friend utterly taken with a paralegal at his office certainly took the prize for botched first advances. After quite a bit of good-natured teasing and flirtation in the office cafeteria, their friendship had blossomed and grown to the point where he felt confident that a light-hearted request for a date would not be out of line. So the lawyer composed a brilliant, romantic, humorously suggestive sonnet to his potential paramour. His serious proposition couched in playful words seemed like a great idea. She could take it as a joke or accept his invite and go out with him. Only he e-mailed it to the wrong address, and his five stanza "Ode to a Paralegal" wound up on a senior partner's computer. (The partner also had a sense of humor, which was why the lawyer did end up dating the paralegal, but not until his poem had circulated by e-mail through the entire firm!)

Disasters like this explain why men appreciate

your sense of humor. Apparently, our fathers used to put lampshades on their heads at parties, though you won't see any evidence of this in family photo albums. Today, when we are smitten, we'll try everything from horrendous Karaoke singing to using highway billboards to attract your attention. And you might as well know that there's a lifetime of occasional foolishness ahead, should you be *the one*.

Laughter is a great antidote to all of our dating faux pas. We dip our ties in our coffee as we suavely flirt with you in the office kitchen. Our voices will crack like preadolescents when we're asking you out. We'll leave you an absurdly ridiculous phone message and then spend half a day *begging* your roommate to run to the apartment and erase it so you don't get the wrong impression when you get home. We get totally nervous when we're courting you and it's a blessed, immeasurable relief to know that you can laugh at our antics—not to mention come up with a few of your own.

Men also notice women who have a great, lighthearted attitude about themselves. Chantal, a Colorado architect, had long, shapely legs and a butt that made her a knockout in a pair of jeans. However, continuing north, she was pretty much flat-chested. She had one particular T-shirt she loved to wear to parties. It was plain white cotton with a beautifully silk-screened *pear* on it. A really nice pear! So nice that *someone* who saw it would inevitably comment, "Say, nice pear!" Well, as corny and silly and utterly predictable as that remark might be, guys just couldn't help laughing when they heard it, and Chantal met more guys because of it. They just had to get to know this flat-chested woman with the nerve to wear a shirt like that!

So, if you want to grab a guy's attention and you're feeling silly, follow Chantal's lead. Have some fun! Wear an outrageous outfit to a party. Use those goofy pickup lines that make us all cringe. Dive into the pool with all your clothes on. Someone is going to be amused! Someone's going to love your playful grin. And some guy is going to think, "Hey, she's funny. I'm going to ask her out!"

Playful Things That Turn Guys' Heads

- Hats (funny, sexy, silly, all kinds!)
- Mickey Mouse underwear
- Line dancing with your girlfriends
- Sixties clothes that remind us of "The Brady Bunch"
- Trying really hard at sports you're not very good at
- Singing old Supremes songs (complete with hand gestures)
- Wrestling with your dog in the park

REALITY CHECK

You're at a party and you meet a guy and he's lively and funny and confident and bold and everything you think you're looking for in a man.

So you go out on a few dates and you start to notice certain things. He is so fearful when he's alone with you that he can barely summon the waiter. He hasn't told a single joke or story since the night he asked you out. His funny, self-assured stories about the workplace have been replaced with nervous mumblings about his intense job. And after three dates this guy you thought was brimming with self-assurance has barely squeezed out a limp handshake before saying goodnight. The big, showy display of bravado he put on to meet you turns out to be nothing but a facade. How disappointing is that? Odds are you won't be having many more dates with a guy who is guilty of such false advertising. And guys feel exactly the same way about a woman who they are getting to know on the first few dates.

Although everyone puts on something of a show when trying to make a great first impression, a man asks you out because he is attracted to you and thinks there may be a future for the two of you. That future might be a second date, or a third; long weekends; stunning sex; a happy relationship; or a marriage proposal, wedding, gorgeous kids, a station wagon and a house in the country. Who knows? But no matter what a man has in mind, he has no doubt placed a fair amount of weight on his first few dates with you and would like you to bear *some* resemblance to the person he originally met.

That's why there are certain things a woman simply should never pretend to be when she is first dating a guy. Don't feign a love of sports, for example, if you despise the sight of any game televised on a Sunday afternoon. You'll be condemning yourself to a lifetime battle against the remote control, a six-pack of beer and a couch full of his best buddies. Don't pass yourself off as a world-class chef if you don't know how to boil water. It puts terrible pressure on you to deliver something that is not in your repertoire, and more often than not, the date turns out to be an uncomfortable failure. Why put yourself through culinary hell when there are so many fine restaurants to go to anyway?

Don't dress like a dominatrix in leather and chains if you're really a sweatshirt-and-jeans girl. For one thing, you're opening the door for a lot of bizarre requests. And for another, if that is totally out of character, you'd probably rather not have to live up to a reputation after the first few dates have faded into a comfortable relationship.

When it comes to what we're looking for in a date, men are not as demanding as popular culture sometimes portrays us. That is not to say we wouldn't enjoy being served cold beers by women clad in leather bikinis on Super Bowl Sunday. It's a nice fantasy. But that's not what most men really want. When we first meet and pursue and date you, we want you to *be yourself*. We stopped dating fantasy women when we threw out the swimsuit posters that hung in our college dorm rooms. Today we want to date women who are confident in themselves. We like that you have jobs and varied interests, and we like your sense of independence. We like your hair any old way you wear it and we like you in thick glasses and cozy sweaters and holey jeans.

Basically, as we get to know you, we want you to do what's most comfortable for you, because that is exactly what *we* are going to do. We'll watch too much TV, belch when we think you can't hear us, stockpile dirty laundry in the corner of a closet and wear our favorite jeans every single day until they're condemned by the health department. Hopefully, we have a few decent attributes to offset our more typically male behavior. In the spirit of fair play, we want to afford you the same luxuries. We don't mind if you sleep until noon, never wear makeup on weekends, and call your mother four nights a week. If we're attracted to you, and that *is* you, we're happy smiling campers. We just want the real picture.

THE SECRET ADMIRER

Karen, a New Yorker and inveterate subway rider, noticed a certain man gazing at her every day on her morning ride to midtown Manhattan. He was cute enough, wore decent suits, and didn't drag his knuckles on the pavement or drool incessantly. Karen was definitely intrigued by this guy. Although concern for her own safety was in the back of her mind (as it always should be), she knew that it was occasionally possible to judge a man by his looks. And she decided that a well-dressed man reading *The Wall Street Journal* who goes to work every morning on the same train probably was not an escaped convict.

So Karen, in need of some new blood in her

tired dating life, started making a point of riding in the same subway car with this man whenever she saw him on the platform. He took the hint. Several times he seemed nearly ready to put down his paper and say hello. But alas, men can be shy and *very* afraid of rejection. What if we asked a woman out and got turned down in front of a car full of subway riders? We'd rather serve hard time than face that humiliation.

This trepidation left it up to Karen to make any sort of subtle move. Finally, one drenchingly rainy morning, she walked out of the subway station one step ahead of her shy suitor and deliberately broke a three-dollar umbrella by opening it too far. As the rain sluiced off her forehead she looked beseechingly to her subway friend (who happened to be opening *his* umbrella, which was about as large as a garden tent). Mercifully, at last, he took the cue, shielded her from the rain and offered to walk her to her office. After a few minutes of chatty conversation, they exchanged work phone numbers.

Although most of the men you'll date won't be as completely unknown to you as Karen's stranger on a train, almost all romances begin with someone playing the role of the secret admirer. Unless your marriage is going to be arranged by tribal elders, at least one person in your potential party of two has to feel that little jolt in the heart and then figure out some clever way to act on it. The streets and offices, grocery stores and health clubs are filled with eligible men and women hopelessly in love with someone they see every day, but have never approached for a date. You're probably in that predicament right now—whether you realize it yet or not.

Wherever your daily routine takes you, there are going to be men who would love to ask you out. So, here are several simple rules for being the recipient of a secret admirer's attention. Obviously, think safety first. Know *something* about the guy: where he works, who his friends are, where he lives. Once you ascertain this man is safe game, drop some subtle hints to let him know you wouldn't mind if he struck up a conversation. A shy smile can work wonders. It says, *"Hi I'm here, but you're going to have to make the first move."* If your not-so-secret-any-longer admirer still doesn't work up the courage, enlist the aid of a friend to loosen him up. At the health club, get a guy friend to talk to him in the locker room. Have an office mate break the ice. Anything to put you and your admirer in close enough physical proximity to be on speaking terms. That way, when he finally finds the nerve, he can comfortably ask you out.

There are more men admiring you from a distance than you can possibly imagine. Every single day, without even realizing it, you're doing something that's probably making a lasting first impression on some man's heart. That doesn't mean you should make goo-goo eyes at every stranger you meet. But if you encounter someone interesting and have some basis for knowing that he has a job, a home and some sort of a life, then that contact could be a safe stepping-stone to a cup of coffee at the company cafeteria, or a stolen slice of pizza on a busy work day. After meeting in a public place, if the chemistry is there, you can decide when and where to learn more about one another and consider the possibility of going out on a real date.

THREE

The First Date

When Harrison, a struggling writer, was slaving over his first novel in a tiny New York apartment, his social life didn't just flag. It died. He figured it was supposed to be this way during his "artistic phase." That was until the day he walked into his publicist sister Leslie's office to meet her for lunch and was greeted by the sight of a pretty woman in jeans, a sweater and cowboy boots, sitting spread-eagled on the floor and stuffing press kits. Harrison immediately queried Leslie about this young woman, and Leslie laughed, not at all surprised that her brother would find her new assistant, Debbie, attractive. Too bad she was unavailable. According to Leslie, Debbie, who hailed from Texas and recently relocated to New York, had already landed a stockbroker boyfriend.

Disappointed, Harrison went back to pounding away at the keys on his word processor. But now he was distracted. The words weren't coming. He had a woman on his mind. He longed to see her again, but couldn't bring himself to call. If Debbie had a steady boyfriend, why bother? "Cute women who date stockbrokers probably wouldn't be interested in hooking up with a starving writer, anyway," Harrison told himself, and he tried to concentrate on his work.

However, every time Harrison called his sister's office, Debbie chatted and laughed and joked with him. They developed a light, easy banter over the phone. Harrison also saw her on several visits to the office, which just confirmed his desire for her. But still he clung to his original supposition, and despite several near bursts of reckless, headstrong confidence, did not ask her out. Harrison assumed that Debbie's flirting must just be platonic repartee, lending credence to just how dense guys can be when it comes to taking hints.

You see, Debbie was very much interested in Harrison. The stockbroker was practically history. But she figured that asking out the boss's brother might not do wonders for her career. Instead she took the subtle route, and dropped every hint in the book. Besides flirting with Harrison on the phone, Debbie questioned him about his dating life every time they spoke (and took the fact that he had none as a good sign for her!). They asked each other what they were doing before the weekend, and traded notes over the phone after the weekend. And still no date. How was Debbie ever going to get this guy to respond?

Finally, she went out and bought a magazine featuring one of his freelance articles, read it, enjoyed it, clipped it, and attached a note: *"Who's the cute guy who wrote this story?"* Then she mailed it to Harrison. Three days later, from a street corner near Carnegie Hall, he nervously called her to ask her if she'd like to go to a concert that weekend.

With a long, deep sigh of relief, Debbie said "Yes." And then proceeded to call every one of her friends to say the lumphead had finally figured it out. She was interested!

Dropping Hints

Have you ever found yourself in a shopping mall, or at the bus stop, or sitting in your car at a light—when you look over at a handsome guy and feel a blush come over your whole body, head to toe? Guys are very well-versed in this feeling, and we are not always so delicate about expressing it—as any woman who has ever strolled past a construction site can tell you. Fortunately, catcalls and rude, two-fingered, ear-splitting whistles are not the only ways men reveal that they are smitten with a woman they've just seen. And the attraction is not always simply a matter of lust. We actually do fall head over heels in love with the way you toss your hair or the cut of your skirt or the twinkle in your eye. The tough part is getting from that instantaneous physical attraction to a first date.

For the woman who is recipient to an interesting man's passing curiosity, dropping a thousand and one hints is one way to test the dating waters. If the man does not respond, you might be disappointed, but you haven't really been rejected or humiliated.

There also might be a good reason why he's not responding as quickly as you'd like. Maybe the timing is wrong. Maybe he's involved with someone else. Or in the middle of breaking things off with an old flame. Or perhaps he's just not in dating mode. (Men have a tendency after a big emotional hurt or during a severe job crisis to turn off the dating switch for a while. We like to take deep breaths and recover our footing, and then jump back into the fray with renewed vigor!)

You can make your interest and availability known to a man just by flirting and fooling around with him. Bring him cookies you baked over the weekend. Anonymously leave daisies on his desk and wander by frequently, smiling every time you walk by. Corner him on a Friday night and lament the fact you're stuck going out with your girlfriends—again! How's that for obvious? Then, give this guy some time to absorb all the information you've been sending his way. Wait and see if he takes the bait. If you're confident there is some small spark of interest but he *still* hasn't asked you out, you can either give up and move on, or change your approach to a more dramatic and risky tactic—asking him out yourself.

Surefire Hints Even Dense Guys Will Notice

1. Tell him how thrilled you are to be out of the crummy relationship you just ended.
2. Ask him to set up, fix or install something of yours.
3. Throw him a compliment. *Nice tie. Great car. New glasses?*
4. Engage him in a highly detailed conversation

about a major sporting event. Drop names. Boast about your knowledge. Mention that your favorite team is in town—tonight!
5. Discuss the weekend weather with him. Make sure he knows exactly where (and when) you'll be in the local park if the sun is shining.

Asking Him Out

Do guys like it when a woman asks them out on a date? Sure. Especially if it's by a sexy, young movie star, or well-known swimsuit model, or the latest hot veejay on MTV. But even if that's not you, we still consider it a terrific compliment. It's nice to be wanted by an attractive and intelligent woman. Does it happen very often? Unfortunately not. It's pretty hard to find couples who can honestly say that their first date was legitimately proposed by the woman ("legitimately" as in directly asking a man she barely knows to go out on a first date with her).

Still, if you're talking to a nice guy you've just met and everyone's heading home and you think you might never see him again—go for it! Ask him if you can call. Ask him if he wants to catch a movie sometime. Ask him if he wants to watch a game with you on Sunday at this very bar where you just met. If he's involved with someone else, chances are he'll break the news right then and there. "Gosh, that's incredibly sweet of you, but I'm sort of, well, uh, engaged!" Honest answer. You can both laugh it off. You'll meet someone else, and he'll spend half his honeymoon wondering about the attractive woman who asked him out right before his wedding day! On the other hand, if he *is* available—chances are he'll agree to see you again. Why wouldn't he?

Men love to be asked out by women we casually meet at a party or gathering. A line as casual as, "Say, we should get together sometime," is a line we pick up on. Then we both trade work phone numbers and the door is open for *either of us* to call. You can wait a week or so to see if he takes the initiative. Or you can dive right in and call him the next morning. Suggest a casual activity, something non-threatening like a walk in the park or an afternoon movie.

If you call the guy a few times and he always has an excuse, figure the timing was wrong and let it go. Maybe he just said "yes" because he didn't know how to say "no." Or maybe he really did like you, but the old girlfriend wasn't quite out of the picture yet. It happens. You don't know this man anyway, so there's no great embarrassment.

A more difficult challenge is deciding how to ask out a man you see on a daily basis, someone from work or your health club, for example. Where do you begin? Start by sizing up the situation. Make sure he doesn't have a serious, steady, or live-in girlfriend. That's easy enough to figure out. Since you talk to this man every day anyway, ask him leading questions—ones that might get him to mention a significant other—such as, "Oh, do you cook?" Men know when they're being queried. If he is in a relationship and senses you're checking him out, he'll answer, "Yeah, I love cooking. Though Marge is better at it than I am." And of course you ask who Marge is and find out he lives with his girlfriend. Onward ho.

Other innocent queries that will help ferret out a man's single status? Try asking him about a weekend hobby: sailing or golf or refinishing furniture. There's a good chance you'll get a clue about how he spends his time, and with whom. Or if you know he goes away a fair amount, try: "Gee you seem to go to Boston a lot. Is that where your family lives?" If he's visiting his fiancée, this ruse will get you the information you need. These ploys may seem devious, but it's safer to figure out whether he has a girlfriend now than to make a fool of yourself by revealing your feelings, asking him out and then having him say, "Gee, I'm involved with someone!" A little clever legwork can go a long way toward sparing you from awkward situations like that.

Once you've established his single status, raise the stakes a bit and do some big-league flirting. Drop hints all over the place. "Say, do you like jazz, because I heard Wynton Marsalis is in town this weekend!" Note: this is *not* asking him out. This is asking him if he likes jazz! It's a fine line, but you're still in the safety zone. If he says he doesn't care for jazz, then it's just a conversational lull, not a rejection.

Other safe opening lines? "Have you been to that new Ethiopian restaurant downtown? I hear it's amazing." Or, "Do you like action films? Have you seen the new Bruce Willis flick yet?" Or how about a simple: "Do you like in-line skating?"

Okay. Now let's say he responds favorably to your in-line skating line. That's where you take the plunge. Assuming the chemistry is good and there's some level of mutual attraction and to the best of your knowledge, he's available, this is where you dance around a good opening line and turn it into a casual date invite. Follow this script.

JUNE

Say, Ward, do you like in-line skating?

WARD

Well, yes I do actually.

JUNE

You know, it's going to be a glorious weekend.

WARD

Really. You don't say?

JUNE

Yeah. You know, I've got these new Rollerblades I was going to try out. If you're not doing anything Sunday, do you want to meet me in the park?

There you have it. A perfect example of a woman *casually* asking a man out on a date. Nothing formal, no big deal. You have not invaded his comfort zone or put him terribly on the spot. If he's an office mate, there is no intimidation or suggestion of harassment. And if he's a friend, you have not made any sort of audacious proposition.

What you *have* done is identified a common

interest—in-line skating—and a good reason to get together—the first spring weekend. You've left him an out—"That's nice of you but I have other plans." And if he likes the idea, you get to skate together in a public park on a beautiful day. If you both have a nice time and it feels right, either of you can suggest dinner or a movie or drinks after skating. Don't want to move that fast? Well, you still have a common interest. You can meet for in-line skating in the park a few more times and see if anything develops from there.

Another way to ask a guy out without being too aggressive or putting your reputation on the line is the "extra ticket" ploy. You just happen to come up with two seats to a ball game and you'd hate to waste one. So you ring the guy on the fourth floor and ask him to go with you that night. It's really tough for a sports fan to say no to that one. Get him to the arena and see what happens.

Then there's the old reliable "group invite." You wander by a man's desk and very casually mention the barbecue you and your old college chums are having down by the lake on Saturday. Then nonchalantly suggest that he bring a Frisbee and a few friends and join your group for a nice, easygoing afternoon. This is a terrific tactic because you're letting him know that you notice him and would like to spend some recreational time with him, but you're also leaving a bit of mystery about the nature of your invitation. If his friends are all busy should he come alone? Are you just trying to get enough people together for a touch football game? How many other guys have you asked? Rest assured, he will be discussing you with his friends and wondering out loud if

The First Date

you were asking him out on a date or just being nice. *You* can decide that for yourself at the picnic.

After You Ask Him Out . . .

WHEN HE SAYS . . .	HE'S PROBABLY THINKING . . .
"A movie Friday night? Can I check my book and get back to you on this?"	*I'm going to call Paula, Jill, Maggie and Jolene first. If none of them are available, I'll try to squeeze you in!*
"Dinner for Tuesday night? You know, I have a really busy week, but what about a drink after work?"	*Oh wow, I never knew you even noticed me! Let's make it cocktails and see if there's any chemistry.*
"Do I want to go to the park Saturday afternoon if it's nice? Sure. Sounds great!"	*I'm so pumped. Better clean the apartment. This could be a big weekend!*

GRABBING THE CHECK

Let me dispel another one of those notorious male myths. No decent guy who pays for an expensive date expects to get some "action" in return for picking up the tab. But what happens when the situation is reversed? If you buy a man an expensive dinner and take him to a show, are you going to demand that he "put out" because you paid? Probably not. (But oh, how we wish!) And now that I've cleared the air on that subject, let's cut right to the chase. If you do the asking, do you do the paying? That can be a rather touchy and complicated issue.

Since asking him out put you in the driver's seat, you *might* want to keep things that way by offering to buy him dinner. It's a statement of sorts. It makes him the recipient of your affection while requesting his attention as a potential boyfriend. The man has to think: Did he have a good time? Was he comfortable being asked out by a woman? Does he want to ask you out next? This certainly sets the stage for a very equal relationship, if that is what you desire.

However, most men will *not* expect you to pay for the centerpiece of a big night on the town (usually dinner), even if you did the asking. It's not that we find *your* picking up the tab embarrassing or emasculating or anything like that (although a few guys still might). Most of us simply are so accustomed to picking up the dinner check that we'll reach for it automatically. It's practically second nature to us.

So, if it's important for you to pay, *you* have to take charge before *we* act out of habit. Perhaps the larger question is, how complete a role reversal do you want when you ask a man out? Will you pick him up at his place? Choose the restaurant? Make the after-dinner plans? Take him home at the end of the night and worry about whether you should kiss *him* goodnight? Then why *not* pay? It's your evening! But it's perfectly understandable if you feel this is too much role reversal for a first date. It's easy to find a less awkward middle ground.

More casual first dates—burgers and beers, pizza and pasta, a movie and a sandwich—leave plenty of room for compromise. You can take charge and plan the whole evening and offer to pay for part of it. If he picks up the movie tickets, you grab dinner. If he insists on paying for dinner, you can buy him a beer at the pub later. It's still your date, but most men will feel most at ease chipping in. The fact you asked him out still makes the experience unique.

Assuming there is good chemistry on this first date, you've established some important ground rules. You've done the initial asking, which means you can ask again. You don't have to sit at home for a month waiting for the phone to ring. You're on equal footing for making future plans. When you've asked a man out once, getting together again is hardly a big deal and that nerve-racking *first* date can naturally segue into a more casual phone call to say: "Watcha doin' tonight? Wanna catch a flick?"

What's On *His* Mind When He Asks *You* Out?

It all begins with a face in the crowd. You like his smile or the cut of his suit. You mumble a greeting on the elevator, and catch a stolen glimpse at the water cooler. A quick joke on line at the company cafeteria, a casual "s'long" as you both race out on a Friday afternoon. It may take weeks of maneuvering to find yourself in a one-on-

one situation with the guy you've had your eye on. Then one day luck, game-playing and sheer coincidence come together like tumblers on a lock—and he finally asks you out!

Having made a compelling argument for the casual date when *you* do the asking, I now have to admit that the whole game changes if the man makes the first move. There is nothing casual about a guy asking you out on a casual date. As a matter of fact, to most guys there is no such thing as a "casual date." If we're just friends, then going out for a movie and a snack is *not* a date. It's just hanging out.

But if there is any kind of chemistry between friends—even a hint of chemistry—then it is *not* casual. We've got something else on our minds. Although I have on occasion known women to accept a date with a guy "just for the heck of it," a man will rarely ask you out *"just for the heck of it."* We might *accept* a date just to be polite or nice. But we won't *initiate* one for that reason.

Every date we go on has special meaning to us. How we ask you out, when we ask you, where we ask you and what we choose to do are all meaningful clues to what is on our minds. Calling a date casual is just a ruse to make sure we don't tip our hand while we explore the possibility of romance with you. This doesn't mean you have to arm yourself to the teeth every time you go out. Men are not the enemy, and you are not the allied forces protecting the fort. After all, we are both purportedly looking for the same thing from a date: the possibility of romance. However, for a guy, dating has to include an element of risk. We want to feel a nervous catch in our throats when our hands accidentally brush against yours at the movie theater. We want to drum our fingers nervously during the lovemaking scene, because we're desperately trying to figure out whether you're picturing us as the lovers on the screen! Maybe you aren't. Maybe you don't feel even a twinge of possible passion. But the fact is when a man asks you out, he does feel this possibility. It is why he asks you out in the first place. And therein lies the key to understanding men's dating habits.

Some men pretend that a first date is not a big deal, but that's far from true for many of us. All our lives we've heard that there is someone special for everyone out there. And we have spent a great deal of time wondering *where* that someone is. Did we date her once and just not realize it at the time? Has she been dropping subtle hints for months and we're just too blind to see? Are relationships like ships in the night that require you to be on the lookout at all times, so that you don't miss seeing someone wonderful out on the horizon? These mysteries and the mere possibility that you could be that wonderful someone makes our first date a very important encounter!

We ask you out because we are interested in something. That "something" might be as straightforward as sex, or as profound as a sign from the heavens that *you* are the one! Generally, our motives fall somewhere between those two lofty principles. And truthfully, for a guy, not knowing where one date will lead is half the fun.

When we first go out with you, we hope that there is some chemistry or connection between us.

We stand in front of a mirror and question everything about ourselves: Do we look good? Are we funny, clever, intelligent, smooth, charming, sophisticated, and passionate when the time is right? And if our date goes nowhere, does it mean something is wrong with us, or simply that this particular date was a bad idea?

If you're reading this and thinking, "Gosh, that's exactly how *I* feel on a first date!", that's great. Despite all the dating game-playing that goes on, men and women's true feelings are probably more alike than either of us ever let on. Do *you* worry that you came on too strong, or made a fool of yourself at last week's party? Well, the guy you met there has probably called seven of your friends to see if you liked him, before he dared dial you directly to ask you out! Do *you* still get nervous about whether you should give him a kiss on a first date? Rest assured *his* heart is also pounding as he fumbles his farewells at your door. Not sure whether *you* should call him the next day to say what a great time you had the night before? Guess what? *He's* sitting at his desk staring at the phone as if it was a poised rattlesnake, hoping it will ring and that you will be at the other end of the line!

Despite sharing a fair number of the same fears and insecurities, men and women are *not* identical in their ways of thinking or communicating. If they were, there wouldn't be so many dating casualties born of miscommunication. The fact is, it can't hurt to understand a man's dating modus operandi. For instance, what is he thinking about while working up the nerve to ask you out? What does each date mean? Does he just pick a time and place helter-skelter, or do guys have a preference? Is there a strategy or game plan for the entire evening?

There are no firm or fast rules. No scientific survey results. And nothing that applies to every man or every situation. Yet there is a certain method to our madness, and understanding where a *man's* head is might help you decide where *yours* should be when going out with a guy for the first time.

The Weekday Dinner Date

When Mike, a Kansas City sports statistician, asked Beth, a registered nurse, out to dinner on a midwinter Wednesday night, he had every intention of taking her straight home afterward. Not because he thought their date would be a loser, but because sometimes when a man really likes you, he'll do exactly the opposite of what you expect. Instead of pushing the evening to the limit or popping a few moves on you, he'll decide to go overboard being a gentleman and politely walk you to the door, give you a peck on the cheek, and call it a night. His heart may be screaming "more, more, more," but his brain says, "Wait. Don't spoil a good thing by seeming overeager or jumping too fast into the fray."

But Mike and Beth got along so well over dinner, and their conversation flowed so easily, and Beth was having such a good time, that *she* didn't want the evening to end. So when Mike offered to take her home, she suggested that if he wasn't too tired (ha!) they could go to a neighborhood bar and watch the Kansas Jayhawks game on TV. As it turned out, Beth was a huge college hoops fan and the Jayhawks were her hometown team. Mike was thrilled. Not only was the date going to continue, which was a delightful surprise for him, but he also learned a valuable tidbit about Beth. She was a real sports fan. A big plus.

When a man asks you out for a weeknight date, you should consider it a very respectable and safe invitation. It doesn't have to be a four-hour evening. It can be a quick snack after work. You can even suggest cocktails instead of dinner. We know what that means. You want to check us out. That's fine. We might feel the same way. That way if our romantic vision turns out to have been somewhat off kilter, we *both* have an easy out. "Thanks for the drink. Bye!" On the other hand, if cocktails go well and the conversation is scintillating, we've already established that we're free for dinner and can continue the date.

Men consider the weekday dinner date an excellent entrée to the dating scene. There are several reasons for this. For starters, it's simple. There's no guesswork involved. We don't have to choose a movie or a play or predetermine your musical preferences (and pray that you like opera because we just invested a C-note in two orchestra seats!) Since everyone eats, we can't go wrong by asking you out for a meal.

Dinner on a weeknight rather than the weekend also eases the pressure to deliver a full-blown primetime evening on the town. No one expects us to make elaborate plans on a Tuesday. That's something we're more comfortable doing *after* we know you! At this early stage, we may not want to invest that much time or money, or for that matter, let on how much we like you.

Also, a first date on a weeknight pretty much precludes staying out until 4 A.M.—which bodes well for you if the guy is overly enthusiastic in his intentions. You have the perfect escape clause. He'll buy it when you tell him you have to go home and get your sleep because tomorrow's a workday!

On the other hand, if that bowl of pasta produces more than just a full stomach and a desire to go home, extending the weekday dinner date sends an enticing message. It lets him know you like being with him so much that you're willing to give up sleep and do something you might not ordinarily do on a weeknight.

Stay Out Past Your Bedtime?
(Late-night Dates We Love)

- Rainy nights at piano jazz clubs
- Sexy midnight foreign films at the art-house theater
- Parking at runway's end to watch airplanes land
- Watching sporting events that originate live from the other side of the world, at a cozy local pub
- All-night ferries against city backdrops (New York, Seattle, San Francisco to name a few)

The Friday Versus Saturday Night Date

Martin, a British bond trader in New York, was a rather well-off man with lots of style and the wallet to match. All his first dates were marked by his cocky attitude and wealthy bravado. And he dated some of Manhattan's most attractive and stylish young women, wining and dining them at trendy restaurants in Tribeca and SoHo. These women were "see and be seen" dates, and when he took them to his favorite pub to "meet his mates," snickers could be heard up and down the bar. These guys were all privy to Martin's legendary Friday night activities, and he always worked the same ruse. He'd bring a nice young woman to meet the "lads at the pub." Then after making her feel like she too was his best pal, he'd whisk her away to his luxury high-rise apartment with terrace view. She would emerge at 7 A.M. on Saturday morning in a wrinkled cocktail dress, shyly looking for a taxi and vaguely aware that this was not the beginning of a long and meaningful relationship.

There may be no medical evidence to support this next claim, but boys' testosterone levels seem to run high on Friday nights. We shoot out of our offices ready for action. No romantic cafés and quiet jazz on TGI Fridays. Something about the work week's end revs our engines, as is evident in the packed, standing-room-only bars in most major cities on a Friday at 7 P.M.

That is not to suggest that women don't also fly out the door of their office looking for action. The fact is, there is something to be said about a release at the end of the long work week and when a man asks you out for a Friday night date, chances are he is feeling bold and purposeful.

When you go out with a man on a Friday night, you can expect a rollicking good time. Bar-hopping. Meeting his friends. Dancing till dawn. Sexy sunrise brunches with you wearing his white oxford and him wearing a tired, contented smile. The possibilities are endless.

While many men do seem to think with their "little heads" on Friday night, every such date isn't guaranteed to end with a randy guy pawing you at your front door. But I'll be honest. Friday seems to bring out the animal in us. It's not a rule. It's not a requirement. It's simply one facet of the male psyche. And it can certainly be a good thing if you're in the same frame of mind.

Saturday night is a whole different creature. When you say "yes" to a Saturday night date, you're saying "yes" to the possibility of real romance. Not the urgent grappling of Friday night, but the practiced machinations of a man who is courting you and loving it!

Saturday night is the night when relationship-minded men polish all their best moves, the ones they've been saving for the right woman. From the moment we hop out of bed that morning, we're psyched about our date! A hundred situps, a hundred pushups, a three-mile run and we're devoting the rest of the day to you! Saturday men buy flowers. They learn to make lasagna. They buy wine instead of beer. On a Saturday night date you can expect to get the red-carpet treatment. We clean our apartments, hide our dirty laundry under the bed, dig out Grandma's fine china. We want to show you that we are capable of living like grownups. It's our way of saying we think you're something special.

Conversation takes on a whole different spin too. Saturday night is confessional night. While the Friday night man regales you with tales of skiing and mountain-climbing and learning to drive a race car, the Saturday night man shares his vision of children and dogs and a farmhouse in Vermont. That doesn't mean you'll be getting a marriage proposal on a third date. But something about Saturday night suggests future and dreams and the distinct possibility that we might be able to share it all with you.

Just in case we have convinced you to let your guard down though, let's not rule out sex. It's not like our hormones take a vacation. They're just repositioned. If the Friday night man is a wild sunrise romp, the Saturday night man is lingering kisses and foreplay until dawn. If this turns out to be the night you make love for the first time, he'll be thrilled you're still in his bed the next morning. But if this isn't "the night" and you slip out the door before it gets light, that's okay too. The Saturday night man will wait until the time is right, because he thinks of a Saturday night date as a road test for life.

Saturday Night Strategy

DON'T	DO
Say yes to dinner at his place unless you really like him.	Bring a really nice bottle of wine. Something special.
Criticize his cooking. At least he's trying to make a nice impression.	Help out in the kitchen if he asks. It's cozy and intimate and a great way to get to know each other.
Schedule anything too early on Sunday morning.	Bring a condom in your purse. You never know!

THE SUNDAY DATE

A friend who lives in a large apartment complex says he fell in love with his current girlfriend in a sub-basement laundry room, meeting her there on a regularly scheduled basis every Sunday morning for three months before they ever went out on a legitimate date. He brought the bagels and newspaper. She brought the laundry soap and fabric softener. *He* knew the style and size of every new bra she bought, and *she* knew that he favored boxer shorts over jockeys. A laundry rendezvous can be the site of many sexy secrets!

Sunday offers a twelve-hour pass from stress,

and a Sunday date is reserved for women we really feel comfortable with. If six days a week our hearts are pounding furiously, the seventh day is a chance for gentle romance. We don't want to work on Sundays any more than you do. We don't want to worry. We don't want to try too hard at anything, and that includes romance. Museums, parks, bicycling, skating, movies, and lazy brunches are all Sunday events. We want to wear our holey jeans, and we want to see you in a sweatsuit without a bit of makeup. A Sunday date can be a mere hour's stroll in the middle of the afternoon or a day-long picnic by a lake. We might not even call to see if you're free until Sunday morning—although we know some women who consider this shabby treatment. Please humor us on this score. It's not that we weren't thinking of you. We might have been dying to see you all weekend. But sometimes we need to surprise you with our behavior. Catch you off guard. Catch our own feelings off guard.

"Impromptu" has its merits. We read about an interesting concert or event in the Sunday paper and we instantly think of you. "I wonder if she'd enjoy that." Or we might be inspired to call by something as simple as a brilliant, sunny spring day. We shoot out of bed, smell the blossoming trees and think: "Hey! I wonder if Monica wants to hang out?"

In truth, men can't pay you a nicer compliment. It's our way of saying, "let's get casual." If you're busy, we understand. But please don't take a last-minute Sunday invite the wrong way. If we're thinking about you on a Sunday, it means we're thinking about you as someone who fits into the cozy, relaxing part of our life. We want to be with you in as natural an environment as possible. And when you say "yes" to a last-minute invitation on a Sunday afternoon, it gives us a tremendous boost of confidence. It says you were thinking about us, too, and that is a good sign.

None of this means that we don't feel passion or romance or lust on a Sunday afternoon. There's no house rule that says the most innocent bike ride can't end up with us scrubbing each other's sweaty bodies in a sensuous midafternoon shower. But on the whole, the Sunday date is a testing ground for more down-to-earth emotions. Spending a peaceful Sunday together is the epitome of sharing quality time.

THE OFFICE DATE

Tim, a Dallas accountant, was deeply, physically and intellectually attracted to Shelley, a fellow numbercruncher at the same stodgy firm, where interoffice dating was forbidden, and being discovered could mean that one or the other might have to leave. Tim was acutely aware of this policy. So instead of leaping into the deep end and asking Shelley out, he resorted to the age-old male habit of lurking! He re-routed his office walks to frequently pass by Shelley's office. He knew her lunch schedule by heart, and always went to the cafeteria for a sandwich at the same time she did. If he learned that she would be working late, he made it a point to work late, too. That proved to be the breakthrough move.

One late night, Tim and Shelley (who were good friends by this time) just happened to be the last two people working. And they just happened to find themselves at the copy machine at midnight. (Men are *so* devious!) Knowing that even accountants get hungry, Tim "casually" asked Shelley if she'd like to grab a bite. She readily agreed. Their office romance began that evening and continued on the sly until they became engaged eight months later and went to the senior partners with their news. Happily, they both retained their jobs and even invited quite a few friends from the firm to their wedding!

There are a lot of politics involved in trying to date someone from the office. Most prominent is the fact that if it doesn't work out (or even worse, if an office date is an unmitigated disaster), we still have to see each other on a daily basis. The other primary concern is the risk of compromising our professional standing because of our personal behavior. Whether it is strictly forbidden or simply frowned on, we don't want to jeopardize our careers trying to ignite a romantic spark with someone at work. Having laid out those caveats, though, let me say that it is true: We sometimes feel an attraction to a co-worker that we simply must act on.

Men have two favorite ways of doing that without actually leaping into a serious date: the business lunch, and drinks after work. Weekday lunch is a particularly safe way to get to know someone outside of work under the auspices of working. Say we're both involved in designing a new format for the company report? It would be absolutely justifiable to spend an hour alone discussing the content and layout and marketing plan for our joint project. Granted, everything we might have to say about work could have been discussed in the conference room. But we want to get out of the office with you. If you have absolutely zero interest in us, then turn down the casual lunch invite. However, if you feel there is even a small kernel of attraction, take a chance and go to lunch. It's a great way to get to know one another on a professional level.

Over the course of an hour away from the office, the conversation is sure to turn to matters other than the project. And if you wander onto the subject of college acquaintances or your love of northern Italian cooking, this is not a crime. If, at any point, you feel that the man is getting too personal, or if you decide that you're not really interested in pursuing anything further with him, start rifling through your sales reports. Make a cell phone call, or six! He'll get the hint and you can both get back to a nice intimate chat about typefaces. No damage done!

Drinks after work is another matter. The invitation begins in the same way. "Want to get together and discuss ol' Phelps' business plan? I know a quiet bar downtown!" In this instance, be sure you like the guy who's asking, because Phelps' business plan is going to become ancient history after one beer. If you might be interested in talking to this man about something other than Phelps' business plan, then take a chance on drinks. See where the evening leads. If you're both having a terrific time, and it's mutually obvious that work is no longer the reason for your being out, then call that evening a nice start to a possible new relationship. But if at any point, for any reason, you simply decide that you want to keep this acquaintance on a professional basis, then you still have your safe and fair "out." Since he asked you out on a work-related basis, this still does not count as an official date, and you have a fast and easy excuse to part ways. "Thanks for talking to me about the project. I've got to call it a night." An intelligent, well-mannered man will get that message clearly and quickly move on.

However, there is one added twist to the *successful* drinks-after-work scenario. If it turns out that you and this man are clearly having a good time, a man will most certainly ask you out right then and there. Why? Opportunity! Lots of guys are emboldened by a lively conversation, or a pleasant turn of events. "Hey, this is great! If you're not busy tonight why don't we continue this over dinner?" At that point, if you accept, you are on a date! But there is a middle ground. You can suggest dinner another time, and then go home to sleep on it. Weigh the pros and cons, and decide if it's prudent to proceed. And if you should decide not to see this man outside work, pull the ripcord. It was still just drinks and a business meeting. You're letting him off the hook gently without crossing any professional boundaries. He might be disappointed, but both of your reputations remain intact. No harm done to either party.

FOUR

Blind Dates: The Agony and the Ecstasy

Mention the words *blind date* to a single guy, and you'll usually elicit a groan. That's because many of them end the way Kevin's did. Kevin, a real *guy's* guy and major sports fan, left a gathering of hockey-loving buddies during a New York Ranger's Stanley Cup telecast to meet the woman a casual female friend had fixed him up with. Thirty minutes later, he was back. Why was his encounter such a brief one?

There are three possible explanations. One: Kevin was such a jerk he couldn't bear to be away from his friends during a sporting event. Two: The Rangers hadn't made the Stanley Cup Finals in his entire lifetime, and nothing less than an audience with the pope could get a diehard fan like Kevin to miss the game. Three: He had broken his own vow to never go on a blind date unless he really trusted the person setting him up. There are few things more awkward and painful than sitting through an evening with someone you absolutely cannot stand—which was precisely what Kevin had been doing. He was having such a thoroughly unpleasant time that he ended the ordeal after one quick drink.

In fairness to Kevin, he did go through the motions of inviting his date to come watch the game with his friends. But apparently the loathing at first sight was mutual. She would have chosen to have root canal surgery rather than spend another second with him! From the sounds of it, Kevin and his ill-fated date were doing one another a big favor by writing off the whole tedious affair.

Not all blind dates have to end so quickly—or so badly. Alene, a dental technician from New Orleans, had much better luck on a blind date that was never meant to amount to anything. At the time, she was engaged to her high-school sweetheart, with a wedding scheduled for the summer after they received their college degrees. Only he went to school in Atlanta, which left Alene alone on most weeknights, and available to do her roommate Mary a big favor on one of them. A man Mary really liked had called at the last second to cancel their date because an out-of-town friend had just dropped by for a surprise visit. They could still go out, Mary told Alene, *if* she would *please, please, please* come along to accompany her date's buddy. Alene reluctantly agreed, although only after learning that Billy, the out-of-town friend, had a girlfriend back home and no more interest in starting a new romance than she did. Two margaritas, one Mexican dinner, and lots of dancing later, she felt differently, and so did he. After three months of surreptitiously dating Billy, Alene called off her engagement and moved to Michigan to be with her new love.

Blind dates tend to strike terror in the hearts of even the boldest singles. There are just so many horror stories about mismatched people trapped in excruciatingly awkward situations that it seems as if they'll never end. Offer to set a man up with a blind date and he'll raise dozens of objections. What if she doesn't have "the look" he likes, or a good sense of humor? What if she doesn't like sports, beer, or pro wrestling? Maybe her idea of a good time will be dramatically different than his. I've been told that women have plenty of reservations, too, and are just as reluctant as we are to go out on blind dates. There *is* an up side to agreeing to one more blind date, though, for women who claim they have sworn them off for life. What could that possibly be?

A man who goes on a blind date is usually willing to consider a relationship. In fact, he is probably *looking* for a relationship. He'll rarely cry "commitment-phobic" or turn out to be too attached to his guy friends to devote time to you. Chances are that he has stopped trying to patch things up with his old girlfriend. And unless you've hooked up with a creep who misrepresented himself in a personal ad, your blind date won't turn out to be married!

Still skeptical? Still wondering why a perfectly nice guy would agree to be fixed up on a blind date? For the same reason you would. Fate has not smiled on his social calendar for a while— perhaps a long while. He is sick of Friday nights out with the guys. He is tired of cooking epicurean feasts—for himself—on Saturday nights. And he doesn't want to wait any longer for sheer coincidence to bring him face-to-face with a nice woman he might like to spend more time with.

Men *and* women who agree to go on blind dates are essentially in the same position. We know there's someone special out there for us, and we know we're not going to meet that person by sitting home alone. We've come to accept that the occasional blind date is better than no date at all. But while we are willing to gamble on going out with a total stranger, we would prefer to avoid an unmitigated disaster. Here are a few choice pointers on how to do so.

Trust Your Mother, Know Your Friends!

Eric, a pleasant enough man from West Los Angeles, had a mother hell-bent on getting him married—and soon! Her pleas for him to find a nice girl and settle down went unheeded by Eric, who was more interested in partying and playing the field. Sure, he would have welcomed a few set-up dates with models or movie stars, or the daughters of movie moguls. One could say his criteria for rating a date were not what you'd call personality based. A relationship-oriented woman would have been wasting her time by going out with Eric at this stage of his life.

If Eric's mother recognized any of this, she didn't clue in Meredith, a 30-year-old talent agent she met at a bar mitzvah. "He's so handsome, so nice, so interesting, and I just know he's going to love you, Meredith!" she insisted as she pressed a cocktail napkin with Eric's phone number written on it into Meredith's hand. Armed with no more background information than this, Meredith kept her promise to Eric's mother and gave him a call. Big mistake!

You see, Eric had no idea his mother was drumming up dates for him (apparently Meredith was the first one to actually pick up the phone), and it was immediately obvious that he had been caught off guard and had no idea why she was calling! Already embarrassed, Meredith figured she might as well go the distance and meet Eric for dinner. Another mistake. From the moment she laid eyes on him in his Armani sports coat and designer T-shirt, she suspected that he was the kind of guy she normally avoided like freeway traffic. As the night wore on, Meredith's misgivings grew.

Eric, a producer's assistant, took her to a trendy Melrose bistro full of glitzy show biz wannabes. She suffered through an expensive plate of froufrou veggies while Eric, the "soon-to-be-a-huge producer," talked on (and on and on) about himself, the people he knew, the movies he had worked on, and the scripts he was purportedly developing for various megastars. Needless to say, Meredith and Eric parted ways after a very brief meal and an even briefer farewell.

Let's face it. Even the most "perfect" relationships are far from perfect. The best-matched twosomes have their differences. Plenty of them. So why should we expect anything different on a blind date?

When playing in the arena of blind dates, both men and women need to face a certain reality: a setup is just an introduction, not a commitment. It is most likely to succeed when you come to it without preconceived notions or an exorbitantly high set of standards. Of course, hoping that your date meets one or two criteria for the kind of person you'd like to go out with is hardly unreasonable. The best bet for avoiding monstrous letdowns is to know and trust the person who is arranging the blind date.

It's a crap shoot to accept a blind date setup in the first place, but the odds are more likely to be against you when the matchmaker is someone you don't know well. That person doesn't know your dating history or plans for the future. You don't know *their* tastes or ideas about what makes a good match. Someone they call handsome, you might find ghoulish. Someone they describe as interesting, you might consider dull as sawdust!

Your safest course of action is to be discriminating from the outset. Your best girlfriend is a safe bet for a fixup, because she's probably been on a few awful blind dates herself and wouldn't wish that on anyone. Your best guy friend is a wonderful source, too. Guys know what guys want. And if you've been honest with them about what *you* want, they'll almost never fix you up with the totally wrong guy. They don't want to hear about it from their friends afterward, and they don't want to hurt you. Your own relatives are fairly reliable—if they know and respect your tastes and intentions. Moms can be a bit of a question mark, though.

On the plus side, your mother won't send you out with a biker if she knows you favor conservative lawyer types. On the other hand, she might set you up with a lawyer when she knows you like bikers. Mothers have a tendency to believe it's their maternal prerogative to fix you up with the man she thinks you should end up with, no matter what you say you want. Even when it's not your own mom, you need to beware. Mothers of single men can be as proud and territorial as your own mom. When a guy's mother corners you at synagogue (i.e. poor Meredith) and virtually extracts a legal commitment from you to call her son, you should contemplate the mother's motives. Who is she setting up this date for: you, the person you'll be going out with, or herself? Does she have the best interests of her son at heart, or weddings and grandchildren for herself on her mind?

Another stumbling block in the fixup department? Beware of setups from friends of friends, or from office acquaintances. Their intentions may be honorable, but they're probably closer to the person they're fixing you up with, and more tuned into his needs than yours. Some will do almost anything to get their lonely companion out on a date and that includes neglecting to tell you certain vital tidbits about him.

For example, you might casually mention that you're a vegetarian and since you feel strongly about it, ask what sort of food your potential date likes. The passing acquaintance who is setting you up might laugh and say, "Oh don't worry about it. He's real easy going. You'll get along fine." That sounds like an answer to your question, which leads you to believe he has the same tastes as you. The next thing you know you're staring at a blood-red ribeye steak on his plate and trying not to throw up—or throw your pasta primavera at him for rattling on about his calf-roping days on the rodeo circuit!

---

5 Crucial Questions to Ask Before Accepting A Setup

1. Has he broken up with a girlfriend within the last month?
2. Does he have a job, and if so, what?
3. Does he live at home or have his own place?
4. Why is he being set up on blind dates?
5. Does he have a bad track record with drink or drugs?

When it comes to a setup from an office mate, you should exercise even more caution. You have more than a couple of hours on a lousy date to lose here. Just how are you going to tell the vice president of personnel that her cousin Matthew has bad breath and probably hasn't bathed in months? And even if you keep your opinions to yourself, how do you know Matthew won't say something awful about *you* to his cousin the vice president? After all, you did knee him in the groin when he tried to ram his tongue down your ear on the movie line! This is one facet of office politics you can avoid. Don't go out with friends or relatives of people who can harm your reputation at work. It's an added pressure you don't want or need on a date—or at the office.

TRUTH IN ADVERTISING

Suppose you're going through the personals and notice an ad that reads: "Well-built, dark-haired, handsome man, financially secure, senior executive of an environmentally conscious company, seeks..." Let's say you respond. Then he calls and sounds as good on the phone as he does on paper. So you agree to a date. Boy, are you going to be miffed when he turns out to be a balding, neckless, barrel-chested truck driver for his brother's two-man garbage hauling business. While there is absolutely nothing wrong with being a truck driver, it's not exactly the bill of goods you thought you were being sold.

When it comes to blind dates, a fair amount of truthfulness benefits everyone—although guys often get into trouble trying to get at it.

Michelle, an Austin, Texas businesswoman had a friend she wanted to set up with her best guy friend, Jeff. He listened attentively as Michelle gave him the lowdown on her girlfriend in broad, general terms: pretty, nice figure, dark hair, interesting job, good personality. He liked what he heard—as far as it went. He just wanted to know one more thing. "Does she have nice breasts?" he inquired. Fortunately for Jeff, Michelle was on the phone and not in the same room with him. Her eardrum-piercing shriek of indignation was enough to convince him that had she been in kicking distance, he would have ended up singing soprano. And deservedly so, you may be thinking.

No woman wants to be judged by her breasts. From her perspective, it's rude, narrow-minded, and unfair. But the way Jeff saw things, it would be unfair *not* to ask. Why? Because, for better or for worse, he was really turned on by a woman with a certain kind of figure, and at the age of thirty-two, with commitment on his mind, he preferred to date women who were at least *close* to the type of woman he liked—whether that was a woman with a 42D bra size, or one who barely filled out a tee.

When you ask about a date *you're* being fixed up with, don't you ask what he looks like? Most women *do* want to know at least the basics, and usually a few specifics as well. For example, if you're five-foot-ten—or just like tall men—would you jump at the chance to date a guy who is five-foot-three? Probably not, and you'd want to know his height ahead of time. (It's better than having your jaw drop in unpleasant surprise staring down at his head when he comes to the door.) You might even get straight to the point and tell your would-be matchmaker that you're just not attracted to anyone under six feet tall. Sure, that may not be fair to half the male population, and by setting that limit you might miss out on a terrific guy who is five-eleven. But you also reduce the risk of disappointment—which, by the way, is why we ask about things like breast size. (Quirky tastes are quirky tastes. Since men and women can't change them, we all have to learn to live with them.)

The dream of all single people who go on blind dates is that they will be smitten at first glance, and blissfully leap from the word "go" into a fantastic, exciting relationship, wondering how they ever got so lucky. While this may not happen in *any* case, the odds are definitely against it if we go out with someone we find physically unappealing in the first place.

What's more, men are visual creatures. If we meet a woman at work or at a party or someplace else where we've had the pleasure to lay eyes on her, we make our moves based on what we've seen. But if we've never seen a woman we're expected to date, we're at a distinct disadvantage and try to make up for it by asking for lots of details about our prospective date's appearance. So please, if a guy you want to fix up with a woman friend does that, don't immediately become defensive or absolutely furious at him for asking. He knows you're doing him a favor and doesn't want to let you down. But no one's going to be any happier if he goes out with your friend *without* knowing what she looks like, and then backs out of a second date because he wasn't physically attracted to her.

When a man *or* a woman agrees to go out on a blind date, they're doing each other a favor by being honest about what they're looking for. Not perfectionist! Not hypercritical! And definitely not cruel. If you or the person you're being fixed up with are going to be too picky, you're probably better off not going on a blind date in the first place. But there is nothing wrong with expressing a desire or preference. Armed with a fairly clear picture of what you *really* want, or know you can't handle, your friend can then use discretion to arrange your date. There is still a risk that once two people are paired up, their attraction will be nil. But at least if both are in the ballpark as far as their likes and dislikes are concerned, there's *some* chance sparks will fly.

Window Shopping

Before giving the green light to a blind date . . .

WOMEN WANT TO KNOW ABOUT HIS:	MEN WANT TO KNOW ABOUT YOUR:
—Height	—Weight
—Hair (does he still have all of his)	—Hair (length and color)
—Eye color	—Eye color
—Physical Fitness	—Figure
—Facial Hair	—Legs

A Perfect Blind Date

Mark and Jeanne, two Boston singles, were set up by an acquaintance who felt they had a lot in common. On the surface it was easy to see why. They both held financial jobs and graduated from Ivy League schools, made handsome salaries and worked tons of hours. After several weeks of trying to find a free evening in their busy work schedules, Mark and Jeanne finally scheduled their blind date at a downtown bar popular with the after work singles crowd. Granted, it was a clichéd meeting spot, but sometimes there is safety in going with the obvious on a first date. The bar can be standard; it's the person who we want to stand out.

Mark arrived first and carved out a spot near the front door so he could keep an eye out for a woman he'd never seen in his life. Based on her description—dark hair pulled back, navy suit, medium height and build—she could have been virtually any woman who walked in for the fifteen minutes he was waiting. Yet somehow Mark and Jeanne recognized each other instantly across the sea of bodies. (Maybe it's just a "look" all blind dates have in their eyes.) Having distinguished one another among the hundreds of other "suits" at the bar, they shook hands and fought their way back into thirty-six square inches of crowded real estate. There were no seats available, so they shouted a conversation at one another over an imported beer, through a thick cloud of smoke.

It may not have been the most romantic of spots to meet, yet after twenty minutes of this charade Mark felt that certain intangible "something" every guy wants to feel on a date—blind date or otherwise. It's just this confident feeling that strikes us and suggests we're going to get along pretty much no matter where we go or what we do. So Mark asked Jeanne if she'd like to lose this crowded singles bar and go elsewhere.

More often than not, if a man feels that sort of

chemistry on a blind date it is because the woman feels it, too. Chemistry is rarely a solo act. And so fortune had it that Jeanne was also feeling good about the evening and readily agreed to get out of the packed bar.

Outside on the cold city street, Mark weighed their various dinner options. They made small talk, shivering in the winter chill, until he suggested a plan. Since their initial meeting had gone so well, they decided to continue their date over dinner in Cambridge, which was closer to both their homes. They jumped on the "T," Boston's subway, and their conversation rambled easily as the train rumbled over a bridge that crossed the Charles River. Heady with the spontaneity of the moment, Mark started thinking that Jeanne was a woman he could kick back, relax, and spend some real time with. He realized that they both were still dressed in stiff suits and weighted down by leather briefcases. Mark decided to take a risk and suggested that he walk Jeanne to her apartment where she could dump her stuff and change clothes while he ran home to do the same. Then they could meet at an informal restaurant to have dinner.

Now, Jeanne could have found Mark's innocuous suggestion presumptuous, or suspect that he was delivering a come-on line. But she was already as comfortable with him as he was with her, so she suggested he come up to her place while she threw on jeans and a sweater. No big deal; it took her all of thirty seconds while Mark politely waited in the living room. Then Jeanne tagged along to his place while he got out of his work clothes. This whole course of events, simple as it may seem, was a real act of trust on Jeanne's part and a pleasant surprise for Mark, who was not accustomed to women inviting him up to their apartments until they had gone out several times. Taking it as a compliment ("Hey, she must be feeling as good about this date as I am") he and Jeanne were soon comfortably dressed and on their way to a Cambridge coffee house for sandwiches and a little folk music.

Jeanne and Mark's blind date was a success on all counts. They were clearly attracted to one another. Their conversation flowed easily from the word go and covered everything from family and friends to workplace woes and career goals. They even got a glimpse of each others' apartments. As a matter of fact, they were so at ease in each other's company that they didn't need to struggle through a lot of the usual, awkward first date stuff. In mere hours they crossed boundaries that take some new couples a dozen dates to break through. Their evening ended with a nice kiss goodnight and a plan to get together on the weekend. A short time later, they were seriously dating.

Like Jeanne and Mark, when you're out on a successful blind date you can quickly discover that you like the person you're with, learn lots about each other in a short time, and generate enough favorable feelings to want to know loads more. This is slightly different than a normal date—although, in either case, falling head over heels in love is preferable to running home and giving up dating for life. A *normal* date comes about after some sort of hook or attraction already exists. You are acquainted with the person you're going out with and you have had enough contact to believe there will be some magic between you.

Blind dates begin one step before that. You and your date have never met or even seen each other, and have only a third party's words or a brief telephone conversation to build on. This lack of familiarity makes us all the more worried that we're going to have an extraordinarily awful time; the kind of date we'll still be flinching from months later.

Some men are so terrified by the prospect of an awkward date with a complete stranger that they won't go on blind dates at all. Others have no time for what is at best a calculated gamble. Most prevalent though are guys who are extraordinarily picky about the women they'll go out with. Men like this can have a potential date's confidential FBI dossier complete with mug shots and fingerprints, and still refuse the fix up. Their only excuse? They didn't choose the person themselves.

Yet, as much as we hem and haw and come up with a thousand and one reasons why no one should ever go on a blind date, lots of men actually love them! Psychologically speaking, it probably ties in to our fondness for undressing women with our eyes. We like unwrapping things and the element of surprise that goes with it. So when Aunt Tamara fixes her nephew up with the nice young woman from her monthly book group, he is truly excited. As he walks to her door his heart is pounding. He can't wait for her to appear. Since he was set up by a relative, he can safely assume that his date is not going to be dressed like a "Baywatch" babe or leather queen. (Relatives never know women who look like that!) But deep down inside he's hoping that his aunt's demure friend in her loose-fitting outfit is actually a smoldering beauty who has been hiding her killer body and sexy ways while waiting for him to come along. (Never underestimate the power of the male fantasy gene!) Granted, reality—at least in the real world of blind dates—is rarely a precise match for our fantasies. But that doesn't mean a blind date can't be fraught with potential, especially if we approach it with an open mind, wanting to like each other and eager to feel a spark.

Assuming two people find one another physically attractive, are there ways to make a blind date a real winner? Most guys say comfort is the key. They want get onto familiar ground with you without unwittingly making the date feel like a job interview. We enjoy talking about the person who fixed us up—this usually breaks the ice. It is the one thing we have in common—and it's always fun to hear how our friend described us. What's more, after playing the geography game (where we both trade university backgrounds and hometown history, and inevitably discover that somewhere in our lives we have a group of friends who intersect), we'll often discover that we have more mutual friends than we initially realized. Bingo—we're no longer strangers!

Another easy opening gambit is talking about previous dating disasters. Like bad-hair days, we've all had them. Regaling us with a few of your best tales from dating hell lets us know that you have a good sense of humor and are open-minded enough to keep picking yourself up and trying again. We don't mind hearing your horror stories. We'll probably tell you a few of our own. And in the process, we'll both learn a thing or two about each other's likes and dislikes.

So, feel free to tell us about the guy who ordered you the hundred-dollar sushi boat at a Japanese restaurant when you despise raw fish. It will save us from making the same gaffe. Have you endured surprise trips to topless beaches, ringside seats for mud wrestling, dove hunting in Texas? We love hearing about all the foolish things our predecessors have done on dates. We are amused and we are educated. And *you* stand a much better chance of avoiding repeat performances of first date faux pas—at least from us!

Winning Moves on a Blind Date

- Dress fun! Great hats, huggable sweaters, your favorite well-worn cowboy boots. What do you have to lose?
- Regale him with your best stories. Scuba diving in the Keys. How you got your private pilot's license. The summer you spent in Greece. Blow him away. This is your one shot!
- If it's a fun date, *you* make the next move. Buy him an ice cream. Suggest a midnight movie. Take him for a drive in your convertible. Night air works wonders.

THE ELECTRONIC DATE

In the 1980s, personal advertisements came into vogue and millions of uncoupled men and women spent a lot of time and money rhapsodizing about themselves and what they desired in a partner on the singles pages of local newspapers and magazines. We learned to decipher the shorthand in those ads and how to separate the truth from exaggeration or complete fabrication. (We also learned to be very careful.) Quite a few of us cringe when we remember a particularly horrendous date that was instigated by a personal ad. Yet, every Valentine's Day there's another TV news feature story about two people who met and married thanks to a personal ad.

Today, we've taken advertising for romance a step further. We log onto the internet and connect with complete strangers through chat groups or carry on slightly more personal conversation through e-mail relationships. The internet has proven to be a great way to share mutual interests with people from around the world. It is a wonderful forum for airing political views, mainstream and otherwise. It is a voyeur's delight for anyone who wants to share his (or her) sexual fantasies without acting them out. But is it possible (or wise) to fall in love with someone in cyberspace? Is this new forum for flirtation safe? At least with a blind date, the person fixing you up knows both parties and has made an educated guess that you might have something in common. Electronic romance requires a great deal of common sense and caution.

If you're corresponding with a stranger by e-mail, ask a lot of questions. Does your e-mail mate have a job? An office? A home or apartment? Anything to verify who he really is? Does he voluntarily bring up the subject of friends or family? If you go so far as to call one another, is his phone number listed? When you call him at work, does a receptionist answer and give a real company's name? You just can't be too careful on this new frontier—which may be why millions of people are making contact on "the Net," but most aren't meeting face to face.

All in all, it's probably not a good idea to go out with a computer contact unless you discover that you have mutual friends who can vouch for you both, or you both belong to a reputable group or organization, where you can meet in the company of acquaintances. If you've linked up through a stamp collecting chat group, for instance, then your safest bet might be to meet at a philatelic convention. If no middle man or neutral, public ground can be found, however, your e-mail romance is probably best kept alive only on the computer.

Caution or Passion?

Most set-up dates start with a safe meeting place and a cautious canvassing of one another; a brief shopping expedition to see if we're interested in the goods. And from a man's point of view, the memorably *good* blind date ends with a laugh and a kiss and a desire to see you again really soon. You were a completely unknown entity several hours ago, and now we're feeling like we'd like to get to know you better. We're thinking: "She's nice. She's pretty. That was a lot of fun. I could like her. I wonder what she looks like naked!" (Even if we don't expect to find out right then and there.) No one goes out on a blind date anticipating fireworks. We're usually just hoping to avert disaster. Occasionally we get more.

Drew, a young Washington, D.C. bureaucrat, and a gang of his buddies were sharing a summer house in Dewey Beach, Delaware, one of the world's great singles gathering spots. Getting "laid" at Dewey Beach is as ubiquitous as finding sand in your sheets. Crowded bars and wild beach-house parties spawn plenty of one-night stands and summer-long flings. However, Drew preferred quiet courtship to arena dating, which may have been why he was drawing blanks on the female companionship front while most of the guys in his house had summer girlfriends. One woman friend took pity on Drew, and arranged a blind date with a housemate of hers who was also turned off by the Dewey Beach animal house scene.

Late one Saturday afternoon, while Dewey Beach rocked, Drew and Nell met for sunset cocktails at a slightly more sedate bar overlooking the bay. They hit it off instantly, sharing dozens of stories of their randy housemates and each new weekend's varied and humorous couplings. With Nell and Drew growing more and more comfortable with one another, cocktails segued into dinner, followed by a moonlit walk on the beach, which ultimately led back to Nell's house where they ended their date tangled in the bedsheets at sunrise. It was the last thing either of them expected, but there was never a question about their affection for one another. And once their afternoon cocktails had blossomed into a twelve-hour gabfest, one could hardly say that they had just jumped into bed. Even though their courtship amounted to one long date, they felt as if they had known each other for weeks.

You'll never hear a guy complain about making love on a first date. (Though he may not always use those exact words to describe the experience.) There's no denying it, though. If you make sex available, most guys are going to leap at the chance. How you are perceived afterwards depends in large measure on the mood of the date. In this instance, Drew *wanted* to meet someone. His heart was in it. Nell's was too. She was a willing recipient of Drew's romantic attentions and a very satisfying summer romance ensued.

Naturally you should always be ultra-cautious about fooling around or going to bed with a man you've met on a blind date. However, caution can be hard to come by when you're caught up in the very thing that can make sex on a blind date so nice: the element of surprise. When you go out with someone you've known a while, you've had time to consider how far you might want to go with that person on your first date; when you might want to head for the bedroom; and what the consequences of lovemaking might be.

With a blind date you don't even expect to like each other, much less *intend* to fool around. You're thinking, "Ugh. Another blind date, another loser evening!" So on that rare occasion when the sparks *do* fly, you're going to be swept away by the unpredictability of it all. *You never dreamed you'd end up here!* And the fact that you have can be a heady elixir. Setting off fireworks may be unavoidable, and as exciting as it gets! But again, even though your body is screaming, "Wow," if your head is saying, "Wait," listen to it. The decent man will call again, regardless of how the first few "goodnight kisses" play out.

A Graceful Exit

So there you are at an elegant restaurant enjoying a delicious dinner with the man your best friend set you up with. He's good-looking, well-mannered and considerate. The conversation hasn't ground to a complete halt at any point during the evening. Only you're bored to tears and faking attentiveness in the worst kind of way. There's nothing wrong with this guy's appearance or his sense of humor. You even think his stories about para-gliding in the Alps are interesting—when you aren't thinking about the load of laundry you left in the dryer, that is, or the novel you'd rather be reading in bed, alone! Well, you're in a spot where we've all found ourselves occasionally: on a perfectly decent date with a generally delightful person you have absolutely no interest in dating. This is not a crime. It is not a sin. But it is a problem, because if one of us knows there's no chance that a romance will be developing, someone has to break the news. And there's really no reliable way to do that without someone getting hurt.

Men are notoriously bad at being the bearer of this sort of bad news. We've perfected any number of methods to avoid coming right out and saying that we're not interested in dating or getting involved with you. Our worst, but alas, most common ploy? Never calling or returning your calls, and hoping that you will eventually get the message we aren't verbalizing. Although this approach infuriates you and earns us labels like bum, creep, liar, or commitment-phobic, deeply flawed individual—we truly believe it is the gentlest and most noble way of letting you down. At least it spares you from hearing our reasons for getting out fast. And really, what else would you have us do?

We could lie. "My ex-girlfriend and I have decided to give it another try." We can hem and haw. "Uhhh, you're really nice and, uhh, I really like you, but uhhh, I'm just not ready for a relationship." That might even be close to the truth. Or we can keep going out with you (sometimes even sleeping with you), until a bad romance eventually self-destructs. This too seems a very painful way to convey a message that we don't like receiving any more than you do. And naturally, we'd rather you didn't use our dubious methods to let us know that you have no interest in dating us, either.

What would we prefer? The truth. (No, actually we hate the truth.) But a man *needs* to know if doesn't have a prayer. He'll *never* assume that his chances for romancing you are nil. If you don't cut him off at the pass he'll act on his natural proclivity to persist. To keep calling. To keep asking you out and on occasion to beg and grovel, blind to the fact that you just don't want to see him.

Charlie, a perfectly nice man having a perfectly lousy run of bad luck, went out on a blind date with Debbie, an absolutely delightful young woman with absolutely no romantic interest in Charlie. Unfortunately, their date went without a hitch as far as Charlie was concerned. They had a great dinner. Debbie agreed to have a nightcap with him at a moody and romantic bar. She even gave him a nice kiss goodnight (as opposed to the hurried race to the door commonly known as "The Rejection Dash!").

The next day, Debbie arrived at work to find a dozen roses waiting for her along with a cheerful voicemail message thanking her for the great date and an invite to go out again that Friday night. Taken aback by all of this before she even had her morning coffee, Debbie called Charlie, thanked him for the flowers and told him she had a nice time too. Then she made a crucial error. Instead of explaining that she was not interested in pursuing the relationship further, she made up an excuse not to see Charlie that Friday night. As a result, for the next three weeks, she had to make up excuses not to see Charlie. Not for dinner, not for Sunday brunch, not to go bicycling by the river, not to meet for cocktails after work, not to join him at a play. Arguably, Charlie should have gotten the message. But he was smitten and willing to roll with the punches until Debbie saw the light. Sadly, the light could have been a nuclear flash and Debbie wouldn't have seen it. She was never going to, and Charlie ended up being very hurt and very disappointed.

If you've been out on a blind date with a man and you know with absolute certainty that it was not just your first date with him but also your last, break the news gently. But break it! Pad the truth. Soften the blow. We don't need an accounting of our every flaw. We don't need a blow-by-blow analysis of what went wrong with our date. Make up a reasonable excuse. "I liked you too, Charlie, but I guess I'm just not ready to date." Or, "Sorry, Charlie. I wish I could tell you I felt the same way as you do, but I'm afraid not. It's not you and it's nothing you did, but I don't think we should pursue this." Even the densest guys will take the hint. Sure, we're going to be hurt and unhappy, but in the long run we'll get over you, and the quicker you break the bad news, the faster we'll move on.

Conversely, the longer you let a man think he has a chance, the harder it's going to be to convince him otherwise. On a date that has no future, we're all better off calling it quits in a simple and honest manner. No need to analyze. No need to pine. We just need a clean break so we can move on to greener pastures.

Lame Excuses Men Use That Should Make You Think Twice

Watch out for these red flags the first time you call him after your blind date.

WHAT HE SAYS:	WHAT IT MEANS:
"Do I want to go away for the weekend with you? Gee, that sounds —interesting—but I'm supposed to visit my Mom and Dad."	*Holy cow, we just met! I'm not ready to share toothbrushes yet.*
"A drink sounds nice, but gosh an old friend just showed up in town. Not a good night."	*It's no one, Trudy. Wrong number. Go back to sleep, honey.*
"I had a really good time too, but I don't know if we're right for each other."	*The sex was great but I ain't the settling kind of guy!*

FIVE

Have You Ever Kissed a Frog?

Are you ready to throw in the towel and give up on dating? Have you had it with the game playing, the small talk, and the failed setups? Do you cringe at the mere thought of another long night out with someone you'd rather not be with? We all have our limits. Maureen, a Los Angeles administrative assistant, and the mother of a six-year-old girl, was way beyond hers. Divorced, stressed out, and about to turn thirty, her views on dating were decidedly bleak. It's hard enough to date when you're twenty-two, just out of college, and full of enthusiasm. Just try firing up your social life when you work ten hours a day, commute almost an hour each way, and have a child to raise by yourself. Most of the guys she had been meeting recently were creeps. And even the ones she liked balked at the idea of dating a woman with a kid.

Fortunately, Maureen had a supportive group of friends who refused to let her wallow in misery for long. A month before her thirtieth birthday, they did something for her that she might never have done herself. They ran a personal ad in a reputable newspaper without telling Maureen what they had done. Then on her birthday, they threw a small party and gave her a sack of mail with almost a hundred letters in it from men who had responded to the ad. Half mortified, half amused, Maureen laughingly took the bundle home, intending to throw it in the trash. But instead she tentatively rifled through the bag, pulled out a few letters, and started reading.

The first few randomly selected responses confirmed Maureen's suspicion that men who answered personal ads were either hustlers and cattle thieves, or lonely guys doing time in local prisons. She was on the verge of ending what appeared to be an exercise in futility when a handwritten note from a man named Robert caught her eye. It was penned on nicely printed personal stationary and included a work phone number where she could reach him. Perhaps it was the gentle rhythm of his words, or the fact that he was divorced too and had a six-year-old son, but Maureen decided to give the letter a second look and tucked it into her briefcase, where it stayed until the following Friday.

As she was wrapping up for the week, Maureen found herself thinking about Robert and on a whim, dialed his number. *He's probably gone for the day,* she thought as she heard the first ring. *It is fairly late. I'll just get his voicemail. Still, it might be intriguing to hear his voice.* A receptionist answered, giving the name of the large company Robert had mentioned in his letter. Good sign. At least he worked where he said he did. Maureen asked for Robert's extension, waited for his recording, and was so startled when a live human answered that she nearly hung up. But something about Robert's voice convinced her not to. Somewhat embarrassed, Maureen haltingly explained who she was and that she had enjoyed his response to her ad. They started talking. Fifteen minutes passed quickly—and much to Maureen's surprise, comfortably. They were soon making plans to get together over the weekend.

When Maureen and her daughter met Robert and his son at a local park, neither adult was particularly impressed by the other's looks. Maureen could best be described as ordinary. And Robert? Well, he was not especially tall. He did not have an especially large amount of hair left on his head. And he wore thick glasses. But Robert was sweet and kind and funny, and perfectly attractive to Maureen. Apparently he felt the same way about her, because by the end of the afternoon, while the kids roller-skated way off in front of them, Robert and Maureen were holding hands and laughing about their good fortune. They even stole a first kiss while the kids weren't looking. A year later they were happily living together.

Sure, men want to date someone with a perfect body, a scintillating personality, and a razor-sharp mind. We'd also like our lovers to be fabulously wealthy, wonderfully adventurous, and unencumbered by demanding jobs or dependent children. But in the real world, there are very few people who fit that description, and we can sit home alone for a long, long time waiting for our dream girl to arrive.

When *you're* lonely and your dating forays have not been producing satisfying results, don't give up. That isn't healthy and it isn't fun. Instead, what if you re-examine your standards and consider adjusting them. Just play with the fine tuning a little bit. When you're wallowing in single-dom, there's no benefit in being ultra-finicky. If you always demand perfection, no one can possibly measure up. The fact is, if you want to have a productive dating existence, it might help to face reality and bring your expectations down to a somewhat more manageable level. Does this mean giving up on everything you've ever dreamed about in a mate? Absolutely not. It just means filling in a few blanks if a man fits some of your expectations, but not necessarily all.

For instance, if a guy has Mel Gibson's smile, but a physique that doesn't quite suit your standard, try finding *something* about his body that excites you. So his butt isn't exactly what you were hoping for. What about his arms? Or his chest? Or something in that terrific smile. There's no rule that says you can't try fantasizing while you make love. Ever so briefly imagining that you're being ravaged by Tom Cruise might add some zest to the moment, *and* net you the fringe benefit of waking up in the morning with a man you're crazy about, who is crazy about you.

Guys have an advantage in this department, thanks to certain traditional male habits—from browsing through "dirty" magazines to picturing ourselves in all sorts of positions with completely inaccessible centerfold models. We learned a long time ago that just because we can't have our centerfold in the flesh, doesn't mean we can't caress her body in our minds or find features of your body that remind us of hers.

So you're a few pounds overweight or have a little bit more of a derriere than we might have chosen? No worries. We're still wild about your breasts. (Haven't you noticed we can't leave them alone?) If you're five-foot-two and we like six-foot women? Not a problem. We'll pretend! Our minds automatically compensate. We fill in the gaps with the mental images we've been collecting for years; visions of breasts and butts and legs and women wearing nothing but high heels while changing the oil in a sports car. (Who knows where that male fantasy came from?!) Regardless, it's the nudity that turns us on. And as a result, we don't *need* you to be one of those magazine girls. You don't have to alter your appearance in any way. If we're in bed with you, it's because we're thrilled to be there.

Men admire a thousand different types of faces and bodies and shapes. And we fall in love for a thousand reasons you couldn't even begin to imagine. By making our romantic goals reachable, we open the door to meeting you, and then we learn to love and enjoy and accept all of you: your mind, your personality, your habits and quirks. By the same token, you'll need to look below the surface and beyond first impressions to figure out if a guy is *the* guy for you. Don't be too quick to judge him by someone else's words alone, or even your own passing glances. If you set aside your preconceived notions of what you *must* have, and try not to judge a man too strictly on every single one of his superficial traits (we all have them!), then you might see his underlying goodness and smartly spend some time really getting to know him.

If all of us would open our eyes a little wider and our hearts a little more, we'd find great catches around every corner. So if your weekend calendar has truly dried up, try spending a little less time hiding behind your job or your personal computer. Go *talk* to the man down the hall. Accept the setup your best friend has been talking about for weeks. And don't be put off if he isn't exactly your type. At least give him the time of day over a cup of coffee or a bite to eat. It's infinitely more fun to be pleasantly surprised, than to write someone off without so much as a chance.

THE SHY GUY

Adam, a six-foot plus computer programmer, had a mind like a bear trap and a body like a lineman. Yet he was still a virgin at age twenty-six. How did this fate befall him? Although no one was offering him a modelling contract, he wasn't ugly. He had a pleasant smile, all of his teeth, and a full head of hair. Adam's problem was that he was painfully, awkwardly shy. Something in his character made it very difficult for him to talk to women. Friends who knew he was struggling found it troubling to watch him at a party. They wondered if he would ever meet a woman who was willing to see beyond his stumbling first impression and give him a chance. Then Gina came along.

As far as dating experience goes, Gina was Adam's polar opposite. There were plenty of lovers in her past, and plenty of fun. More than enough. Dating up a storm has its down side, though, as Gina discovered. A few too many wild nights on the town, and a few too many weekends away with guys she barely knew (and liked even less), had left her jaded and incredibly lonely. Gina completely stopped dating. She devoted herself to her job as a teacher and got involved with a local charity, donating her time to help troubled kids in the community.

When a mutual friend introduced Gina to Adam, their only common ground seemed to be the fact that they weren't dating anyone else, and neither expected much to come of their date. Gina was exceptionally low-key about it. And for Adam, whose extreme shyness had caused such problems in the past, the pressure to impress Gina was minimal since she had already agreed to go out with him. Basically, neither had any expectations.

They met for coffee. That's all. One iced cappucino. So they talked for a few minutes and had a few laughs and found themselves getting on well enough to make the big move. They got their free refills! Gina and Adam ended up talking and laughing the afternoon away. By this time, completely wired on coffees, they agreed to go out again. From there they delicately and carefully and very slowly progressed from a trusting friendship to a dating relationship.

Time and trust proved to be a magic potion for them. When they finally (and mercifully for

Adam) became lovers, their initial forays into sex were bold and exciting. Although they were coming from vastly different bases of experience, this served to cement their romance, rather than making it a difficult fit. In the final tally, two seemingly mismatched people found a perfectly happy and harmonious relationship.

Are you only interested in the smooth guys? The ones dripping with insincere charm? The ones who pick up women as easily as picking up their laundry, and discard them just as readily? Where has this exclusivity gotten you? How much worse could you do by considering the quiet guy, the shy guy, the nerdy guy, and so on? They are not *trying* to be goofy or awkward or tongue-tied. The computer nerd might actually be a very interesting person, or a terrific, innovative lover. Sometimes he just needs a small vote of confidence—perhaps a few easygoing dates—to come out of his shell and demonstrate qualities you'd never have guessed about him.

Dating is an imperfect science. It's impossible to tell at first glance who will fall short in the romantic long run, or carry you over the finish line. So it can't hurt to pay a little more attention to the reserved guy. He might have as much to offer as the playboy. And if you're patient and encourage him to strut his stuff, there may be all sorts of enticing secrets just waiting to be unlocked by the right woman.

Can You Date Your Best Friend?

Leslie and Don had been buddies since their college days. Over the years they had partied together, gotten drunk together, danced together, even traveled through Europe together, sharing cramped beds in youth hostels and nodding off on each other's shoulders in tiny train compartments. But they had never entertained the notion of sharing a romantic kiss.

When mutual friends announced their engagement, Leslie and Don became the last singles in their gang of college buddies—and fair game for every would-be matchmaker at the wedding in St. Louis. They were introduced to cousins and nephews, compelled to dance with business partners and bridesmaids, and eyeballed for fix-ups with friends and relatives who weren't even at the reception. But when the long, champagne-drenched celebration finally ended, they once again found themselves alone, together, crawling out of a rented tuxedo and hideous bridesmaid gown in the hotel room they were sharing to defray the costs of the wedding weekend.

Leslie, wound up from the all-day ordeal, took a long, hot bath before bed while Don, slightly tipsy and stripped down to his boxer shorts, lay wide awake on his side of the mile-wide king-sized bed. He looked up as Leslie emerged from the bathroom wearing a fluffy terrycloth bathrobe and toweling dry her long hair. When she hit the bed with an exhausted sigh, Don offered to rub her back. No ulterior motives. No preconceived notions. But as he kneaded her shoulders and rubbed her neck in the flickering light of late-night TV, something came over him. What began as a soothing backrub turned into a sensuous rubdown followed by a passionate kiss. Had long-simmering chemistry finally come to a boil? Did they suddenly feel older and wiser and somehow closer? Or was it simply the setting? Whatever the impetus, many hours later, two friends lay sound asleep in each others' arms as new lovers. (And not one of their longtime companions was surprised when they came to brunch the next day holding hands. Apparently this was one setup that had been so obvious that no one had dared suggest it!)

It has been said that dating a friend is like kissing your sister (or brother). And I'm sure it's true in some cases, but as Leslie and Don discovered, not all. If you are a single woman with a super-close guy friend for whom you feel the slightest attraction, take a second look. Review the history of your relationship. Have you ever felt something—*anything*—toward him? Are you physically attracted to him? Even mildly? Can you imagine kissing him? If the answer to any of these questions is "yes," (or would be if you didn't think the guy in question would laugh you right out of town), don't rule out your best guy friend as a boyfriend.

There's a certain logic to this. You've known him long enough to trust him. You're already on speaking terms with one another's friends and family. He's probably closer to you than any guy you've ever dated—close enough for you both to be aware of each other's wants and desires.

Of course the sex part might be a stretch for you, but most men are not going to be quite as shy about considering you as a potential sex partner. One of our best-kept secrets is that we are quite capable of falling in love with our female best friend. We would definitely consider having sex with her and have probably fantasized about it more often than she'll ever want to know. We always hold back, though, because we don't want to ruin the friendship.

So, if the only thing separating you and your best guy friend from a fantastic relationship is sex, maybe you need to give the matter more thought and perhaps test the waters to see if he's interested. Obviously it's going to be awkward at first. He's so used to you scoffing at his sexual exploits and aspirations that he may never make the first move. On the other hand, he might also be uncomfortable if you tried to seduce him like any old guy you just met at a party. Very likely he'd laugh and think you were kidding.

However, if you find yourself in a potentially compromising situation (like sharing a hotel room at a friend's wedding), or a potentially romantic situation (a summer sunset walk on a lonely beach), why not physically or otherwise gently hint that you would be receptive to a move on his part? How can you do this? A gentle squeeze of a hand. A certain way you look in his eyes. Mussing his hair or stroking his cheek in a manner that suggests romance more than playfulness. You don't have to tackle him on the beach and kiss him into submission. But the subtle hint that his attentions would not be unwelcome could really put a new spin on an old friendship. You just might find that a man you've always called your "buddy" can be a lot more.

Is There More than Friendship on His Mind?

WHEN HE SAYS:	WHAT IT MEANS:
"Well if we never meet the right person, we can always marry each other."	*I'd stop dating today if you'd kiss me just once. When are you going to come around?!*
"Don't cry. That guy was a creep anyway. Why don't you stay at my place tonight?"	*She's really upset. If she'd let me comfort her, I know we'd hit it off and sparks would fly!*
"Everyone thinks we'd make a great couple. Isn't that the funniest thing you've ever heard?"	*You're the only one who doesn't know it. C'mon, let's get naked and see if they're right.*

"WOUNDED IN LOVE SEEKS FRIEND IN NEED . . ."

A guy walks in on his fiancée doing the horizontal cha-cha with one of his groomsmen. On his wedding day! Say nothing of it? Just a bad break? Get the ring back, get the hell out and get on with your life? That's what men are *supposed* to do when they get their hearts broken, right? Unfortunately, it's not always that easy. What about you? Have the last half-dozen men you've met wooed you, wined you, dined you, made love to you, and then run off with your best girlfriend? Big deal? Try to forget about it? Remove that friend's number from your rolodex, then move on? Not likely!

Ted, an attractive Phoenix home construction contractor in his late twenties, had his heart skewered, removed and handed to him on a silver platter by Suzanne, a woman he had been dating for more than a year. Ted had asked her to move in with him, and Suzanne had readily agreed—right before she went off to the Arizona mountains on a week-long camping trip with several friends. While Suzanne was out negotiating wooded trails, Ted was negotiating with condominium rental agents. He found a reasonably priced duplex that met their specifications exactly, and he couldn't wait to show it to Suzanne. Unfortunately, she had found something that met her exact specifications as well—a young, burly woodsman with his own rustic lodge by a lake. Suzanne never came home. And Ted was so devastated he couldn't even look at a steep incline without picturing Suzanne with her mountain man and feeling sick.

Meanwhile, back in the city, Stephanie, a slim, sexy secretary at an insurance company, was deeply, madly, painfully in love with one of her division's executives. Throughout their torrid affair, she had dreamed about settling down with her lover, a dog, and the house with the white picket fence.

Unfortunately, her executive paramour was dreaming about bedding virtually every college coed doing a summer internship at the company—and his dreams always came true. When Stephanie realized this, she quit her job, found temporary work, and gave up dating for the rest of her life. Or so she told her best friend, Rhonda.

Enter Yenta the matchmaker, in the guise of Rhonda. She knew Ted. She knew Stephanie. She knew they shared a lot of similar interests. And she knew they were both wallowing in self pity. As far as Rhonda could tell, it was a perfect match. Too bad they both adamantly refused to be fixed up. So Rhonda, whom no one would ever accuse of being subtle, threw a dinner party for six couples and the intended twosome. Ted met Stephanie. Stephanie met Ted. And they ended up going out for a drink after the party.

This wasn't an official date. Neither planned for anything to come of it. But after a beer or two, their sob stories started to slip out. Stephanie admitted that she had been humiliated recently, and wasn't really interested in dating anyone for a long while. A decade sounded like a safe time span. Touched by her revelations, Ted shared *his* latest misadventure. He too held romance in rather low esteem and felt this might be a good time to take up a hobby, like learning Homer in the original Greek. Ted and Stephanie commiserated, cried on each others' shoulders, and slowly, one step at a time, re-established their confidence in romance. With each other!

Good manners and prevailing mores suggest that men and women should not trade notes on loves lost. But when you think about it, what unites jilted lovers more than the rotten experiences they have in common? When we've been crushed by a lover, why *should* we take a deep breath, keep a stiff upper lip, and lie to every new date we go on? What is the merit of convincing a stranger that we're tough as nails? Why should our mothers or psychiatrists be the only ones to hear our sad stories?

Joining the lonely hearts' club doesn't guarantee that you'll meet someone immediately, or that the someone you meet is going to be your "perfect match." Sometimes it just feels good to air those grievances to a date. Not for twenty-seven dinners in a row. And not if one or both of us is truly in need of professional help. Mentioning that you think all men are rotten and there isn't a good one left in the entire city—just two minutes after you meet your date—may not be such a great idea. You certainly don't want to hear about a man's lifelong love who ran off with the pro baseball player—five minutes after he picks you up. But if you've *both* lost at love and can find a common bond in your similar experiences, why not talk about them? Share a little comfort and commiseration. It may convince both of you to stick your toes in the shallow end again, and try your luck again, together.

When Love Hurts . . .

DO	DON'T
Go easy on the gory details when you talk about heartbreak on a date. Just give him enough to know you're human, and in need of a trusting friend.	Go on for three hours complete with lengthy sobbing jags. You'll scare a lot of guys off that way, and they'll never believe you're over the last guy!

DO	DON'T
Accept his hugs, his shoulder, maybe a tender kiss. His sincere gestures may be just the cure you need.	Sleep with him to forget or get back at your ex. Not only does this strategy never work, but it's not the way you want to start a hopeful, *new* romance.
Listen sympathetically to *his* tale of woe. It's a positive step that he wants to confide in you.	Overidentify and then launch into a tirade against his ex. Commiseration is good, but a vendetta is unneccessary.

A Mismatch Made in Heaven

Ed, an architect who liked fast cars, fast women, and late nights on the town, hadn't held down a decent relationship in several years. His friend Kristin wanted to change that and offered to set him up with a new friend of hers, Marta. Time and time again, Ed balked. He suspected that Marta, whom he knew held a politically correct job with an environmental protection group, would prove to be a "granola queen in a burlap sack." He had already decided that she favored art museums and afternoon tea, and would have absolutely nothing in common with the martini-and-night-life kind of guy he fancied himself to be. However, his friend persisted for so long that he finally agreed to *one* date. Just one, and only to get Kristin off his back!

This was pretty much Marta's attitude, too. Having heard that Ed was a slick playboy with an enormous ego, she was fully prepared to clash with him from the word *go*—which just goes to show how wrong two people can sometimes be. Ed and Marta went out to dinner on a Monday after work (is there a night that ranks lower on the romantic date scale?) and quickly discovered that they actually shared many of the same political views, appreciated the same avant-garde music, and were active volunteers for the Special Olympics. As a result, a pairing that looked improbable on paper, became more pleasurable with each passing moment. Not long after their first fix-up, Ed and Marta started dating steadily.

We all have a tendency to pursue members of the opposite sex with whom we hope to have something in common. When friends set us up, the obvious is usually the connection they look for as well: Chuck likes sports, Renée likes sports. Tony likes the ballet, Margaret likes the ballet. So they'll probably like each other. It's perfectly natural to think so, but not foolproof. When you've been in a dating dry spell, insisting that there be clear, compelling, common ground before you so much as sip latté with a guy can be a bit limiting.

If every man you've dated for the past year has fit your common-ground criteria—same look, same income level, same hobbies, same sexual habits—and none of those relationships worked out, maybe it's time to be a bit more flexible and open-minded. Opposites can attract if you give them a chance.

Patty, a tall, willowy waitress and acting student, was big on adventure, but a stranger to commitment. Her idea of a meaningful date was rehearsing lines with a pony-tailed classmate, followed by sweaty sex in a fifth floor walkup. Her idea of a long relationship was if she saw the guy again.

Martin, a tall, athletic sales executive, had a health club membership, a closet full of expensive suits, a harried day job and barely enough time to microwave dinner before calling it a night. *His* idea of a date was squeezing in a meal at a trendy restaurant with a client. His idea of sex was hopefully with someone besides himself. Let's just say he was in a bit of a dry spell.

A hundred mutual friends wouldn't have dreamed of setting Martin and Patty up on a date. They had about as much in common as Bob Dole and Madonna. Yet, they met at a party six months ago and have been in a heady and healthy relationship ever since. How did they become so wrapped up in one another? What is their secret?

Because of their separate schedules, they hardly ever see each other during the week (which does wonders for the sex life!). They have separate friends and rarely mix his business associates with her theater acquaintances. They also steadfastly refuse to discuss their work lives during their leisure time.

However, Martin takes Patty to every Broadway play he can get tickets for. Patty, a passionate chef, cooks Martin elaborate, romantic gourmet meals on their Saturday nights at home. And they in-line skate and jog and work out together every weekend. When they're not devoting hours to making up for lost time apart by making love several times on a weekend morning, they inhale every syllable of the Sunday paper over leisurely brunches that stretch on until late in the afternoon. Not such a bad relationship for two such seemingly mismatched people, now is it?

So what if a man you meet is a card-carrying conservative and you're a dyed-in-the-wool liberal. You're not running for office together. You're just going out to dinner! Or what about this typical male scenario: *He* claims to be the world's most devoted golfer, and *she* thinks that the links are sausages. Is that really a reason not to go out? Sure, if he's looking for a caddie instead of a girlfriend. Many of the details that convince us to eliminate our opposites as possible dates are, in reality, the most peripheral of traits. Someone who looks like your opposite from the outside may actually be someone who will run independently in some areas, and be passionately by your side in others. Who can ask for a more perfect match than that?

10 Things A Guy Might Enjoy If You Pushed Him

1. Classical music
2. Cooking
3. Impressionist art
4. Vegetarian food
5. Letting you drive
6. Shopping for clothes
7. French films
8. Ballroom dancing
9. Jane Austen
10. NCAA Women's Basketball

THE FINE ART OF COMPROMISE

Doug and Rosemary were both from the same small town in the northeast, and met at a friend's pool party. The attraction was immediate, but there was one small problem. He was a textile manufacturer working for a clothing company in Singapore, and she was an engineer stationed in Tel Aviv. The good news was that their jobs were both with international divisions of U.S. companies that provided generous travel allowances and large blocks of time in which to use them. Their eighteen-hour journeys between Tel Aviv and Singapore gave new meaning to the term "long-distance dating." Yet, remarkably, their romance blossomed.

After a year, Doug and Rosemary decided they wanted to live together. The question was, where?

Eventually, they came up with an equitable plan. They would continue in their respective jobs on opposite sides of the globe for six months, while Doug finished his assignment. Then he would transfer to London, where Rosemary's company had a large division. They would live there for a year with Rosemary dividing her time between the Tel Aviv and London offices. Then they would reevaluate and decide whether they wanted to settle in Europe, Asia or Israel. Now that's compromise!

So, he likes action movies. You like foreign films. He likes to ski. You like the beach. He's into Indian food. You love Chinese. This doesn't mean your budding relationship is ill-fated. But if it's going to work out, are *you* going to have to learn to love curry? Will *he* have to give up Aspen in February to spend a week with you in St. Thomas? Should you resign yourself to seeing every Jean Claude Van Damme movie that comes out? Maybe, maybe not.

Compromise is the key to any successful relationship, and the inability to meet somewhere in the middle will be a relationship's undoing every time. Consequently, if you're not in a romance at the moment, this might be a good time to look back at your past affairs. Have you given halfway decent relationships enough time to get off the ground? Did you start out with realistic expectations? And if there was a conflict, were you able—or willing—to bend?

Cindy and Jay, a Baltimore couple, had dated through the winter, and their romance was gaining a fair amount of momentum when summer's arrival threatened to cause a major rift between them. You see, Jay was a passionate sailor, but

Cindy couldn't even look at his boat without getting seasick. And Cindy adored the beach, while Jay found lying in hot sand with oil all over his body to be an excruciatingly boring and pointless pursuit. They tried alternating weekends together, one on the boat, one on the beach, and wound up miserable. For a while it looked as if their relationship might crash and burn. Fortunately, they found a happy middle ground. Jay joined a sailing club closer to the beach and spent his days sailing. Cindy rented a nearby beach house with her girlfriends and enjoyed the sun and surf. At night Jay either entertained Cindy and her girlfriends on his boat (not a bad deal in any guy's mind), or abandoned his boat to spend the evening with Cindy at her beach house.

How to spend weekends can become a real sore spot, especially if the two of you have dramatically different interests. In Jay and Cindy's case, they averted a potential romance-ending crisis by respecting each other's desires and finding a way to each do what they loved at least some of the time. It's all in the attitude, really. There's no need to give up lifelong hobbies or change your system of values.

Of course, if your idea of fun is an Audubon Society outing and your guy wants to take you duck hunting, the gap may be unbridgeable. But it behooves us both not to jump to that conclusion and exit the relationship without trying to work out a mutually agreeable solution. We need to give ourselves a chance to *reach* these impasses. We can always bail out of a new relationship *after* it becomes undeniably clear that we're both headed in completely different directions. But there are few things sadder than looking back on some of our better "almost-relationships" and realizing that they might not have ended, or might have ended more amicably if we had only been a little more forgiving or open-minded.

Overall, compromise in dating is like the effects of eating garlicky clam sauce on a dinner date. If one person eats it and the other doesn't, you have a smelly problem. If neither of you tries it, you have no idea what you're missing. But if you both give it a shot, you have a shared experience and a problem solved.

ONE LAST PITCH FOR THE DIAMOND IN THE ROUGH

He's out there. You may think you'll never find him, but he is definitely aware of *your* presence. He saw you on the subway or spotted you buying a diet soda at the kiosk where he gets his newspaper every morning. He's been sitting down the hall from you at work for the past six months. You just haven't noticed him, and he hasn't worked up the nerve to talk to you. Yet! Maybe the opportunity hasn't presented itself, but he'd love to ask you out.

The man who is out there for you knows the aching, lonely feeling of being dateless on yet another weekend. Like you, he's tired of cooking for himself (and halving and quartering recipes, or filling his freezers with leftovers from meals he ate alone!). He jogs solo in the park too, gazing jealously at couples running in tandem. But he's not giving up. Why? Because the old adage is true: there's someone out there for everyone.

Melanie, a researcher at an Atlanta high-tech

firm, wore thick glasses and unflattering clothes, and spent long hours in front of her computer gnawing on a pencil and twirling her hair. While her co-workers were out carousing at happy hour on a Friday night, Melanie worked late and went home alone. However, she did not go unnoticed. Tim, a quirky 22-year-old who favored loud ties and black sneakers to the standard corporate uniform, was new at his job. From the first day he logged onto his computer, Melanie intrigued him. But every time he was about to approach her, one of his new, jockish work buddies would appear with news of yet another trendy party.

Tim continued to admire Melanie from a distance, until one Friday night he begged off from going out with his established group of friends, and stayed at work late instead. In no time, he and Melanie were the only two people left in the office tapping away at their computer keyboards.

When Tim couldn't stand it any longer, he pushed back his chair, worked up his nerve, and asked Melanie point-blank: "Do you want to go out with me?" There was silence for a good ten seconds in the dead-empty office before Melanie's priceless response: "You mean me?"

Were this a romance novel, this would be the part where Melanie pulled the rubber band from her hair, shaking out her long, flowing tresses. The two would fall into a clinch on the boss's desk, and young Tim would find that beneath her frumpy clothes, Melanie was hiding an awesome figure. Then they'd make exhilarating love six times before collapsing on the carpeted floor. Sorry to report, such was not the case. Melanie was precisely as plain as she seemed at first look. And that was just fine by Tim. They went out for a bite to eat, talked about semiconductor manufacturing and its effect on the environment over a glass of iced tea, and discovered that they had both graduated from engineering programs at prestigious institutes of technology. Tim and Melanie started dating and were living together three months later.

If you haven't been on a good date in months, and the last six guys you went out with were creeps, and if you're afraid to say yes to any more invites because your recent dating experience has been so disappointing, here's some advice: Smile at the diamond in the rough. It actually feels pretty good to surprise a guy who isn't expecting it by showering him with a little attention. See if he smiles back. See if it leads to a chat or a conversation or a sandwich in the office cafeteria. Go slowly, one step at a time. Give the friendship a chance. Don't even worry about whether it leads to a date.

If it does, there's no guarantee that a date with this man will be the be-all and end-all of love and sex and romance. If you turn out to be completely wrong for each other, you've lost nothing. But in the crazy, confusing, mixed-up world of dating, there's always the chance that the next man you say "hi" to will be the one. But you're not going to know—and he's not going to know—unless one of you takes a chance and says hello!

SIX

Sex!

Roberta, a conservative-thinking and usually conservatively dressed social worker, was dating Mike, a staid department store manager. They had been going out for two months and their dates had been very low key. A few cocktails-after-work meetings. Several nice dinners. An evening at the movies. A most traditional courtship conducted with the utmost of manners and civility. Other than a few lingering kisses outside the door to her high-rise apartment building, their passion had been mostly of the smoldering variety, although Mike was definitely longing to see what lay beneath Roberta's reserved personality, not to mention her stylish, but relatively unrevealing clothes. The fact that her manner of dressing showed so little—and left so much to his imagination—turned him on all the more. (Contrary to many people's opinions, tight-fitting minis, high heels, and bustiers are not the only outfits men go for!)

Thus far, all of Mike's time with Roberta had been formal and fun but totally asexual. She had turned down any overtures that might have gotten them into his apartment. And he was starting to think that he might be taking cold showers after every stimulating date well into the foreseeable future. The thought did not thrill him. Like most men, he was programmed to think that he should be the one to make the first move. But he also believed that dating for a month or two without even finding himself in a position to share more than a goodnight kiss was a good reason to question whether his date was really attracted to him or not.

Fortunately, fate stepped in where Mike's best ploys had failed. Roberta had agreed to play in a Saturday afternoon charity softball game, and on the spur of the moment, she invited Mike to join her. This would be the first time they had gotten together on a weekend day when they could wear something other than business or dress clothes, and Mike was totally psyched by the prospect of being with the usually prim and proper Roberta in a rowdy, relaxed setting. Call it the "librarian syndrome" if you will. He was so taken by the sight of Roberta in a polo shirt, chino shorts, sneakers and a ballcap that he could barely concentrate on the softball game. Her casual look and fresh-faced sexuality, so dramatically different than the protective, professional cocoon she so often wrapped herself in, excited Mike tremendously. And all the moreso when the skies opened up, drenching everyone and cancelling the game.

Mike drove Roberta back to her apartment building and he was going to head straight home himself to change into dry clothes, but impulsively, Roberta invited Mike to come upstairs to her place and dry off. She threw him a fluffy towel and an oversized University of Nebraska T-shirt, then disappeared into her bedroom. As the rain beat down against the windows, Mike peeled off his shirt, dried his soaking body, and wandered around checking out various details and minutiae of Roberta's life: pictures of her family and sheepdog; knickknacks in her tiny kitchen (we can learn tons about you in fifteen seconds by studying your refrigerator magnets); the CDs on her stereo rack; the books on her shelves.

Mike was standing by her bookshelf, perusing a dusty copy of *The Brothers Karamazov,* when he was startled by the touch of a warm hand on his bare shoulder. Roberta, barefooted and bathrobed with her wet hair pulled back in a rubber band, laughed at his startled reaction. Then, grabbing the towel from his hand, she did something extraordinarily (and unintentionally) intimate. She dried his hair. As Mike stood facing her, their bodies nearly touching, she threw the towel over his head and rubbed and kneaded and massaged his head before pulling the towel away and making a futile attempt to comb his mussed hair with her fingers. Then she handed him the T-shirt he had somehow dropped onto the floor, and disappeared back into the bedroom.

Being a typical guy, Mike was quite thrown off his gameplan by Roberta's sudden and unexpected show of affection. But before his mind could react to his body's sudden urgings, Roberta reappeared in her jeans and a sweatshirt. On her initiative, they ordered a large pizza with the works and rented a couple of videos, which she and Mike spent a romantic afternoon watching together, squooshed up on the sofa stealing the occasional kiss. No racy boundaries were crossed and no bare skin caressed (that afternoon), but in Mike's mind that first time in Roberta's apartment was a great sexual experience!

Mental Foreplay

Every guy has heard it a hundred times: *Men think with their little heads!* But this is not necessarily the only male truth. Sometimes our little head is just the rudder. It's our big head that's captaining the ship. And it is largely our imagination that drives us into a frenzy of sexual desire. When you wear that especially sexy little dress to a party on a Saturday night, and capture the attention of every guy you pass on your way to get a Perrier, it is not simple animal desire that makes them want to have sex with you right there on top of the buffet table. No, when men are attracted to a woman, we think about sex on a hundred different levels. We want to kiss you and seduce you and undress you and tease you and do everything in our power to drive you wild, hopefully while you're doing the same to us. Granted, all these seductive scenarios eventually end with sexual intercourse. But then, that *is* the end of it for a guy, at least for a little while.

Once we've actually done it with you and we've both collapsed in a sweaty, breathless heap, we either have to get out or pass out, leave or sleep, depending on how far our relationship has come. That's one reason why the real fun for many men is in the buildup—the moves and maneuvers and near misses leading up to lovemaking.

When we are first dating you, there is nothing more exciting than the mental undressing of your body and soul. You are a puzzle waiting to be solved, a gift waiting to be opened. And that's how a decent man with a kind heart and a patient spirit will treat you. This doesn't mean you have to feign modesty to entice a man any more than a man has to fake spontaneity. We *have* been hoping and planning for and fantasizing about having sex with you. However, men are not as obvious as we are often portrayed. We do occasionally, even frequently, think with our hearts and minds. And when we are thinking with that *other* part of our body, our ideas about what is or isn't sexy are as unique and varied as the way we make love. We can think of hundreds of ways for you to seduce us. Stolen kisses on lazy walks. A squeezed hand during a romantic movie. Being surprised with flowers after a nice first date. Receiving a suggestive note or an unexpected touch that promises more. More *what?* Who knows? The purpose of mental foreplay is to keep two people guessing while they're getting to know one another. When you whet our sexual appetite with provocative little hints, we keep calling and asking you out and wondering what's beneath your alluring facade.

10 Things Men Fantasize About Before They've Ever Kissed You

1. Oral sex (both ways)
2. Your breasts
3. Undressing you
4. Your orgasm
5. Doing it in an unusual place
6. Food games (think syrup or honey on your body)
7. Doggie style
8. Mutual masturbation
9. Wet T-shirt contests (especially if you're shy)
10. You and your best friend

WHOSE MOVE IS IT NOW?

Okay. You're absolutely crazy about this guy! You've flirted with him at the office and sat next to him at lunch, quizzed all his work buddies and dropped enough hints to rouse the dead. Finally, he worked up the nerve to ask you out. Now you're sitting across from him at a romantic restaurant. Conversation is crackling. The ambience is perfect. So, as the waiter pours you each another glass of wine, are you mentally undressing him? Picturing his muscular chest? Wondering if he wears boxers or briefs? As he tells some fascinating story about his college days, are you imagining him naked with your lips running over his neck, his abs, and more? As he butters a dinner roll, are you visualizing him peeling off your underwear and slowly, deliberately, and sensually making love to you—right there on the linen tablecloth in front of the whole restaurant? Well, whether you're imagining this or not, there's an excellent chance your date is, which probably doesn't come as a huge shock.

When a man asks you out—even before he asks you out—he has probably imagined every inch of your naked body in every conceivable way. As a matter of fact, that may be one of the factors that drove him to ask you out in the first place. Rest assured, while he was looking you over from afar, his eyes held nothing but admiration. He only hoped you would feel as turned on by him as he was by you.

With the possible exception of the Super Bowl, sex is our favorite game. Of course, we only get to *watch* the Super Bowl. With a willing partner, we actually get to play at this sex thing. That is, if we can decipher the rules and come to some consensus on who wants what, when and from whom. Obviously if there is instantaneous combustion and the sparks are flying and we can't keep our hands off each other, time and place may be easy to figure out. It's right there and right then. (Although on a first date, we rarely know each other well enough to jump each others' bones quite so quickly.)

Assuming our first date does *not* erupt into spontaneous foreplay, though, there is little more delicate, yet delectable in the dating game than the rituals leading to sex. Not just sexual intercourse, but foreplay, fooling around, making out, or whatever you consider sexy. When it comes to sex, men and women seem to agree on only two things:

First, unbridled passion is good. Second, being safe is mandatory. Everything else is open to interpretation. Sadly, guys today are as much in the dark about your wants and desires as we were when we first attempted to unsnap your bra in our Dad's car (and as you might recall, we would have had an easier time performing microsurgery than figuring out how to maneuver those impossible tiny backhooks with one trembling hand!). In this age of supposed sexual equality and political correctness, we are bombarded by a cacophony of contradictory voices talking to us. We hardly know how to respond. Be aggressive. *Go easy.* Make the first move. *Wait for your lead.* Be spontaneous. *Don't touch me there.* Talk about each sexual plateau with you. *"Just shut up and kiss me!"*

The rules of the game have changed. Men used to think they were the only ones who felt that diehard, aching lust on a first or second date. But in many discussions with modern thinking women, I've learned that there are times when they would welcome a little more heat on a date themselves. As Kris, a Houston physical therapist, puts it, this dilemma occurs when she's very attracted to a man and, "my hormones are fighting with my brain!"

Unfortunately, the expectations and pressures men feel have remained pretty much the same. It's true, we are no longer shocked by a woman who makes the first move. We have, on occasion, heard dirty little nothings whispered into our ear and happily obliged the whisperer. But the majority of men will tell you that under most circumstances they still feel that it will be a snowy day in July before a woman initiates lovemaking. And despite the fact that both men and women *say* they are interested in an open, honest, vibrant sexual relationship, it often seems as if *men's* open, honest, vibrant sexual desires are targets for criticism. Among other things, we're regularly accused of having nothing but sex on our minds.

But maybe that's because our minds are filled with so many questions about the current mores of sexual etiquette. For instance, since it's still more common for men to take the initiative when it comes to "fooling around," if we're out on a date with you and the mutual attraction is there, when do you want us to make a play? Should we kiss you on the first date? Are we wimps if we don't? Do you prefer moves that are bold and aggressive, or subtle and laid back? How are we supposed to know when you are aching for us to seduce you? And when you *are* being sexual and seductive and somewhat aggressive, how can we tell if you do or don't want us to think, "anything goes"?

George, a pilot for a West Coast commuter airline, had gone out on several dates with Tricia, an airport reservations agent at one of his regular destinations. Their mutual attraction had been confirmed by a heated kissing session that ended with George going back to his hotel alone before flying out the next morning. Then one night, Tricia offered to cook George dinner at her place. There was candlelight and wine and soft music. They ended up dancing in her living room and kissing in the apartment complex's hot tub. Eventually it got so late that Tricia invited George to stay over. Heated up both literally and figuratively, George accepted Tricia's invitation. When they got back to her apartment, she disappeared into the bedroom. George took it as a promising sign and waited patiently for a few minutes, prepared to make the big move. Finally, dressed only in his soaking wet boxer shorts (which were doing little to hide his enthusiasm), he tapped lightly on Tricia's bedroom door. A moment later she appeared, dressed in the world's grungiest sweats and carrying an armful of bedding for the sleeper sofa! Not only was George's passionate mood instantly doused, but Tricia was good and steamed at his presumably "outlandish" assumption that she would even *consider* letting him cross the threshold of her bedroom on a third date. A heated argument followed. Tricia felt taken advantage of and George felt misled. He threw on his clothes, went back to his hotel, and they never saw each other again.

Should Tricia have slept with George that night just because he had a burning desire and an obvious problem in his boxers? Of course not! But inviting a date to sleep over after drinking a bottle of wine with him and then passionately kissing in a hot tub, probably wasn't the best idea either. By leaving their intentions unspoken, they created a typical—and typically tragic—communication breakdown.

Perhaps while Tricia and George were groping in the hot tub, she could have planted a kiss in his ear and invited him to stay the night—with the caveat that he would sleep on the couch! Then their foreplay could have gone on unabated. They might have fooled around for hours and maybe even ended up in Tricia's bed anyway. But having laid out the ground rules *ahead of time,* if bed was not an option on this date, George would have known his boundaries and been expected to respect them. If he did not, Tricia would have had every right to boot him straight out the door!

No one wants to sacrifice spontaneity, but in sexual matters men wouldn't mind receiving a bit more encouragement and coaching from your camp. We'd love it if more women were more direct when talking to us (or hinting at us) about their sexual expectations and desires. Like George, we often could use some help in figuring out the rules for our particular courtships. Give us clues when we're moving at the right clip, and firmly (but gently) let us know when you want us to stop. Yes, you've been doing that for eons, since junior high, in fact. Back then you practically ripped our shoulders out of the socket if we reached for your breast. And that's a gesture we clearly understand. However, two adults who respect one another but aren't yet sleeping together should be able to get their message across in a slightly more sophisticated manner.

Try straight talk. We can handle it as long as it doesn't come off like a lecture from the school principal. You don't need to pull out a sheet of paper and read us our rights every time we get intimate. ("You have the right to caress my breast on the third date. You have the right to unsnap my jeans on alternate Saturdays if the moon is full. You have the right to get horizontal on my sofa as long as your boxers stay on at all times.") That's a bit extreme. There are sexy ways to let us know what you might want to do with us some day, although not right at this minute. Whispered promises. Sensuous mumblings. Amazing kisses with the prospect of more, when you say you're ready. These are enticements that can be quite effective. And it wouldn't be the worst thing for both of us to talk about our hopes and intentions in a forthright manner, just so we have a general idea of where we're going.

When we're first getting to know you sexually, we don't want to act like buffoons and make fools of ourselves. Granted, there are some guys who are truly pigs, but we hope they're the exception, not the rule. Most men are simply looking for the same thing you are: a safe, mutually satisfying sexual experience. So, if we promise to treat you with respect, might you occasionally behave a little less respectfully? Can we both strive to keep sex fun and exciting and spontaneous, while still maintaining a sense of decorum and decency and of course, safe and mutually agreeable behavior?

If we make some effort to keep our testosterone in check, and you occasionally take us by the hand and tell us what's right for now and what might be right later, we can probably find a nice, sexy middle ground that satisfies both our desires of the moment and our hopes for the future.

If You Want to Seduce Him

DO	DON'T
Invite him back to your place. Go for the first kiss if you think the time is right.	Attack him like a pro wrestler the second he crosses the threshold of your home. If he agreed to come in, he's not rushing anywhere.

DO	DON'T
Get out of your work clothes or suit if you feel like it and put on something you consider inviting and comfortable (a loose-fitting, untucked flannel shirt for example).	Feel compelled to come out of your bedroom dressed like a B-movie stripper. Some guys might like that, but many others might find it silly or contrived.
Take charge in your own digs. You pour the wine, you pick the tunes, you make the moves.	Feel like you have to go all the way. It's your party and you should only go as far as you want it to.

THE INFINITE POSSIBILITIES

Green eyes. Dark hair. Women with glasses. Shared showers on Sunday mornings. Naked breasts. Great butts. Long wet kisses in glass elevators. Miniskirts and high heels. Cowboy boots and jeans. A meaningful squeeze in a public place. Making love on an empty beach. The curl of your lip or the jauntiness of your step. When it comes to what really turns a guy on, the possibilities are infinite—and extraordinarily individual. For every man who lusts after the lingerie-and-lace type, there is another man wowed by the girl-next-door look. Some guys melt over blondes; others exclusively give chase to redheads. Brainy intellectual versus fun-loving party girl? There's a man for every type. There is only one incontrovertible truth you can count on. When we ask you out on a date, we are already turned on. We probably don't know why. And it probably isn't the result of anything you did deliberately. Maybe we caught a fleeting glimpse of you bending over to drink from the water fountain. Perhaps we were blindsided by the sound of your voice when you said "hello" on your way past our cubicle. Regardless, when we pick you up for that Saturday night date, our heart is pounding and our minds are racing with visions of what might happen next.

At a certain point in the dating process, a man knows that the romance is going somewhere. He can feel the sexual tension increasing. It's palpable. You pick up on it, too. It may have taken a dozen dates or more to get here, but now the relationship is about to turn sexual. Some of you will want guys to suddenly become smooth Casanovas and seduce you with rakish glances and manly gestures. But you'll be pleased to know that men don't have sexual standards we expect *you* to live up to by a certain date. We consider *every* step of the way fun. We don't have a preconceived notion of what is sexy. "Fooling around" can run the full gamut, from a long kiss under a lone streetlight to extensive foreplay with our clothes strewn about and hanging like drying laundry from every corner of your apartment. There are no set rules and no right ways. What we like is the exploration and the chase.

Men salivate at the mere thought of good things to come. So, if you have a personal code of ethics that says you don't sleep with a guy for three months no matter what, then tease him with the promise of what might be—if he is smart enough to stick around. There are plenty of ways to stoke a man's fires without compromising your values or deflating his passion. Drag him to the hottest club in town and seduce him on the dance floor with your body and your kisses and your whispers. Tell him what you like, and how you like it, as you grab his butt and slow dance the night away. Tempt his mind and his body will follow. Kiss him goodnight like there's no tomorrow and rest assured, as he's driving home he'll be thinking about the softness of your lips and the scent of your hair, the sexy things you said and all that he's looking forward to the next time he sees you.

Or consider this woman's unusual style, who brought her date back to her apartment one night after dinner and a movie and did something he had never had happen before. There had been a lot of heat (and a little action) on their first couple of dates, so this man was definitely looking forward to what might happen next. They had just started fooling around on the couch, when the phone rang. The woman took the call, which turned out to be from a close friend who lived across the country. After several minutes of conversation, the woman started talking about her date, as he sat there listening. She described his looks and his face and clothes and hair—*and* what they had supposedly done right before the phone rang. She made him keep absolutely silent while she spun an utterly sensual, lurid, exquisitely graphic, completely fabricated tale. It was a full sexual recounting of events that had not happened. Yet! The man recalls the experience as a fantasy come true. When the woman finally said goodbye to her girlfriend, she gave her guy a knowing smile and they returned to their fooling around. That night, she eventually made him go home. But this man knew what was in store. And he knew he was dating a woman who definitely was not shy. Evenings like that rank high on the sexy rating scale. It's precisely the sort of titillation that keeps men coming back again and again.

The First Time

Andy, a 25-year-old Oregon park ranger, had been dating Joan, a divorced store clerk, for about six months. Their relationship had started off slowly. A few nice walks, a movie, a few dinners out, a concert. The "dating" aspects of their romance were going fine, but sexually, except for a few long, fumbling kisses on Joan's doorstep, the well was pretty much coming up dry. Was there some sort of problem? Not exactly. It was just that Andy had not had sex in quite a while, thanks mainly to his last girlfriend who apparently possessed about six personalities, with at least three different ones manifesting themselves in bed. Her often bizarre sexual demands had taken their toll on his libido, and he was more than happy to take things slowly with Joan, who was still adjusting to single living after being unhappily married for seven years.

Joan, who had just turned thirty, was not especially concerned about the snail's pace at which their physical relationship was moving. She liked Andy and was attracted to him. She wasn't in a hurry to leap into bed with anyone. To this day both she and Andy can remember every excruciatingly slow, extraordinarily sensual early sexual experience they shared: the first time they kissed, the first time he felt her naked breast beneath her blouse, and the first time he felt *her* bare hand sending shivers across his naked chest. Never wandering beyond removing one article of clothing at most, they were behaving like two high-school virgins, and enjoying every minute of it.

After months of this extended foreplay, Andy and Joan finally slept together—during a camping trip to Yosemite National Park. On their first night there, they both shyly undressed away from the light of the fire, and wearing only their underwear, crawled into a double sleeping bag together. They slowly, gently, haltingly explored each other's bodies, knowing exactly where they were headed. When Joan finally reached down Andy's shorts, however, their initial attempt at lovemaking came to a climax—well—immediately. This is something every man has experienced at least once, and far from being a disaster, it barely broke the rhythm of their foreplay. Twenty minutes later a resuscitated Andy made love to Joan for the first time, beginning what turned out to be a memorable weekend of sensational sex in every conceivable hideaway the trails and lakes of Yosemite had to offer!

This tale is not intended as a paean to premature ejaculation, but rather a tribute to complete, uncontrollable arousal. Having waited so long to make love to Joan, Andy was so incredibly turned on that he literally couldn't wait another second. Women often are able to turn us on like that and they can be equally responsive to our touch, which we find almost unendurably exciting. When we're seducing you and we find a spot on your body that sends you into paroxysms of pleasure, we won't mind it one bit when you can't control yourself. Have an orgasm while you're fully dressed. Have three! Men love it when anything (or everything) sets you off. Of course, we won't find your buttons, and you won't find ours, and neither of us will figure out how to push them by reading an instruction manual. We both need to talk, to move slowly, and to explore.

For most men, exploration, anticipation, and titillation are everything. When dating turns to foreplay and your hands and his are wandering and both of your clothes are coming off article by article, stop and take a deep breath. Slow down. Spend another minute on his neck, and his chest. And that sexy thing you did to the palm of his hand fifteen minutes ago? Do it again. Whatever sends shivers down your spine is likely to send shivers down his. We can happily camp out for a week on your soft breasts or spend an entire night nuzzling your neck, and we savor it when you do the same for us.

When the time is finally right to make love, we're hoping for more of the same slow, sensual pace. The three-minute, frantic, clothes-ripping pool table sex scene may have its place (usually on the big screen), and if the sparks fly the first time, we'll definitely sign up for it again. You just won't see too many men refusing wild uninhibited sex (and no matter how much fun we're having galloping to climax, we'll briefly interrupt to put on a condom). However, men are also ardent supporters of slow, tantalizing, passionate lovemaking. We want to worship every inch of your body from head to toe, and that takes time. We want to savor every detail of the moment, painstakingly undress you, and slowly, methodically make you squirm and twist and squeal and giggle and laugh and have an amazingly memorable experience. And we want you to administer that same sort of attention to us. If we've dated this long while holding back our natural desires, why hurry to the end of the act? Coax us, seduce us, build us up then slow us down. And when we both can't control ourselves another second, obviously the time is right. The first time. The second time. And every time after that, because when we enjoy sex with you that much, you can always bank on us returning for many encores.

However, what if the first few times are not the stuff of legend? What if you're nervous, or he's overanxious, and the sex just isn't amazing? How do guys deal with this occasional problem?

Like all touchy dating situations, it depends on the man. If he blames you, makes fun of you, or simply withdraws without talking to you—lose him immediately. No questions asked. He's not mature enough to get involved in a serious sexual relationship. Write the whole affair off to miscommunication and absolutely do not blame yourself. Good sex is a team effort, and that is the decent man's credo in overcoming a less-than-memorable beginning to an affair.

There are two keys for a guy to join you in taking an average sexual first encounter to greater heights: understanding and laughter. The understanding comes when you both acknowledge that these first forays are experimental—like seasoning a good stew—and you both have to discuss your tastes, and keep trying, until the flavor gets closer to your liking. The second key is laughter. Plain and simple, we both have to be able to laugh during sex. Why? Because sex can be very funny, especially when it's such a new experience. You're urgently trying to peel each other's jeans off over cowboy boots and you both trip over one another with your pants down around your knees? Yes, it looks ridiculous! And yes, you can laugh, take a deep breath, and slow down. He's located *his* favorite sensitive spot on your body, but it happens to be *your* most ticklish spot? When you're done quivering from the giggles, just help him find a slightly less touchy zone. And what if he can't quite get that condom on properly in the dark in a foreign bed, and it's making him want to scream or cry? Take his hand, take the condom and help him out. Awkward situations need only be uncomfortable if either of you take them too seriously. If you both can smile about something—anything—you choose to do in bed, then you can build on the first halting steps and turn them into a confident sexual relationship.

Sexy Moves That Drive Us Crazy

- Make love with only an unbuttoned oxford shirt on.
- Whisper something ultra-sexy when he least expects it.
- Show *him* how to touch *you,* slowly and sensually.
- Find an imaginative use for hand cream.

- Go out with no underwear on. Tell him in a very public place.
- Keep a small bottle of sweet liqueur handy. Apply to sensitive body parts (yours or his). Make sure no one leaves a drop behind.
- Slow dance naked with him while he's fully dressed. *You* decide if and when his clothes come off!

THE MORNING AFTER

Crunch time! This is what separates the boys from the men. You can learn more about a guy ninety seconds after the first time you have sexual intercourse with him than you've learned on all your previous dates. Why? Because we suddenly feel vulnerable. Exposed. Heck, we're naked. And we're naked with you right beside us, skin to skin. While that often makes *you* all cozy and warm, it sometimes makes *us* all jangly and disoriented. Especially if we're in your apartment!

If it's midnight and you've just collapsed on each others' spent bodies, and he suddenly bolts upright in bed, throws on his clothes, and runs out the door, let him. Sit there with your arms crossed for five minutes. If he doesn't come running back with his head down, sheepishly begging your forgiveness, lose this guy. No matter how cute he is or how good the sex was, he is not ready for anything that remotely resembles an ongoing relationship. Nice guys don't bail out ten minutes after ejaculation! Of course, you also should worry if your date bursts into gut-wrenching tears immediately following his orgasm and clings to your neck like a drowning man. He's probably not over his ex-girlfriend yet. Unless you want to be the bounce-back lover, just allow him his one night's respite from loneliness and then tell him to come back when he's ready to be with *you*—not the ghost of a past lover. You don't have to be too harsh about this, but the fact is if you are the first woman to sleep with a man since another woman broke his heart, your heart could get tromped on next. What's more, a guy on the rebound might be far less attentive to your needs than he is to mending his own wounds. Best to give him time to sort things out before you get too involved.

These two extremes always spell trouble. But even when neither of us is quite so selfish or needy, things can get tricky the morning after our first time. There is something about making love that invariably changes the way men and women relate to each other. New lovers may even fall into unexpected roles, acting much different than they did while merely dating. See that cute guy sound asleep in the bed next to you—the one with the adorable dimples and boyish grin? Any minute now, he might wake up sounding a bit *too* grown up; a bit like your father. New sex does funny things to some boys. All of a sudden he'll want to fix the faucet on your bathroom sink, discuss your stock portfolio, or change the oil in your car! Frightening, but true.

After courtship turns a couple into lovers, some men will become overly enthusiastic about their budding relationship with you. We feel as if we're running the hundred-yard hurdles, and now that we've cleared the final obstacle by making love with you, we're dashing for the finish line. Sometimes you have to take our hand and let us know we can slow down. Don't kick your new lover out the door because he's talking about building you new bookshelves two minutes after you've climaxed. Simply and gently convey to him that there's no hurry, and you'd be happier if he took things a bit more slowly.

When you wake up in *his* place for the first time, he may be the one applying the brakes. Lying there beside you, he's apt to feel a little out-of-sorts. Not necessarily bad. Just a bit foreign. It's unusual to see a lovely, naked woman in the spot previously occupied by dirty laundry, a pet dog, or last week's pizza. *You* are a vast improvement, of course. But your presence still takes a little getting used to. We're just feeling a bit awkward. Chances are, you are too. But don't be bashful. We'll usually welcome a good-morning kiss or a good-morning cuddle, or if we're both feeling randy, a good-morning roll in the hay!

More sex is always nice, and it's even better if last night's lovemaking had that wonderful out-of-body sensation to it—the kind of encounter that has us both thinking, "Is this really happening to me?" If we're already lying on our backs staring at the ceiling with contented grins on our faces, another go could only enhance this supremely blissful moment in our new relationship. It reaffirms the experience we had last night.

What negates that experience, and annoys lots of men, is the woman who feels she has to bolt back to her apartment the instant the sun comes up. Dates who behave this way always seem as if they're trying to deny that last night ever happened. And that makes men feel crummy! If your hasty exit is the result of first-time jitters, or wanting to get a grasp of the situation and take things slowly—we can certainly respect your feelings. But understand ours—which shouldn't be difficult since you've probably felt them yourself. When you leap out of bed as if you've been stung by a bee, hurriedly dress, offer a quick peck on the cheek, and run out of our lives, we feel hurt. Used. Cheap. As if we did something bad. We're not asking you to hang out for every remaining second of the weekend. You don't even have to stay for breakfast. But please realize that when we like you, we can be sensitive to the way you leave.

As you're getting ready to say good-bye, we're going to feel as nervous as you do. It's absolutely natural. Our lovemaking changes the way we deal with one another. The relationship is different now, and the moment you walk out the door, we're going to be thinking about that, and perhaps worrying about it. We're only trying to stretch out the morning after with you, because the night before was so special. The very first time we make love is a no-repeat performance, and we want to squeeze every ounce of goodness out of it!

Of course we understand if you *have* to go because you have other plans. We both have lives, and neither of us may have expected to find ourselves in bed together on Sunday morning. But even if you are booked for the rest of the day and must leave, at least let us walk you out or buy you breakfast at the local diner. Just a hurried cup of coffee feels nice and gives us a sense of closure on the date.

However, the *nicest* way many men can think of to end a wonderful Saturday night date that culminated with first-time lovemaking is to spend Sunday morning with you. There is a sense of otherworldliness to the "first time," and rather than run and hide from those initial feelings, we'd really like to build on them. Let's get bagels and read the paper in bed. Or fall back asleep and wake up together again—just for fun! We love it when you use our shower and come out wearing our bathrobe, your hair still dripping wet and your makeup gone. That's the real you and it's really sexy—which doesn't mean we have to have sex again. When we're feeling this good on a Sunday morning, you can bet there will be plenty of opportunities to make love again in the future.

A FEW NOTEWORTHY HIGHLIGHTS

We know you don't want us talking about all the intimate details of our relationship in the locker room. So for argument's sake, let's assume the man you're dating would never dream of such uncouth behavior. But in the back of your mind, have you ever wondered what kind of sexual behavior might cause men to regale their buddies with tales of their good fortune?

Vocal women seem to get a lot of good press, as in, "Hey Mikey, I had a real screamer last night!" Men clearly get a kick out of uncontrollable squeals. Lets us know we're doing something right, and that turns us on big league!

Anything public is definitely appreciated and duly noted. One friend told a story about getting a "foot job" from a date in a fancy restaurant. Of course, we don't have that on videotape (and you can take all these locker room stories with a grain of salt), but suffice it to say, the prospect will keep a lot of men staring under the tables of couples near them. Men love it when you go down on them in taxicabs or give handjobs in movie theaters—anything that rings of danger and the potential of being discovered. Maybe it's because so many guys had their first sexual experiences knowing that a cop could shine a flashlight into the car at any moment. ("Hey buddy, watcha think you're doing there?") Or perhaps it's because our adolescent fumblings were interrupted by a sleepy mother wandering downstairs ("Is that you, son? Is there someone with you?" *"No Ma. Just me and Fido wrestling on the couch. Go back to bed!"*). We were raised on the risk of exposure, so there is an aphrodisiacal quality to fooling around in public places.

Elevator sex. Wild displays of self-gratification. Talking dirty. We do notice a sexually adventurous woman, and these are all sexual adventures that could make you stand out in a crowd. However, you don't have to buy out the sex shelf of your local bookstore. There are plenty of less outrageous ways to make a lasting impression.

Shower sex is a safe, good (clean) bet for turning a man on. If you've just spent your first night together at your place, and he's thinking about leaving, offer him a towel and steer him to your shower. Give him about three minutes to luxuriate by himself, then surprise him. Two bodies under pulsating streams of water are a very good thing. So are soapy hands in new places and scrubbing each other to our hearts' content.

New positions and new places always spruce up the traditional routine (and creative new places often demand exciting new positions!). Some of the better ones? The kitchen chopping block à la *The Postman Always Rings Twice*. The swimming pool (score bonus points if it's in your public apartment complex pool after hours!). And believe it or not, your living room sofa. So often we get all hot and bothered and make a beeline to the bedroom. Well, a bed is fine, and you won't hear men complaining about it. But what the sofa has that the bed does not is arms. Use your imagination and try a few new positions using this sexy prop.

Please note: The key thing to remember as you're opening the doors to a sexual relationship is to *do only what you feel comfortable with*. For all the bawdy male joking about wild sex, we are more interested in developing a relationship with you than starring in an X-rated video. Memorable sex can be making out for an hour on a moonlit pier. Or just curling up naked together for the very first time. When we grow comfortable as lovers, we can explore as many new avenues as we desire. But our heart has to lead for our bodies to follow.

10 Places Where We'd Love to Fool Around

1. The beach at midnight
2. Elevators
3. Back row of a crowded movie theater
4. Anything with four wheels
5. The bedroom you grew up in
6. Airplanes
7. The diving board at a public pool
8. An outdoor terrace with a city view
9. Your office desk
10. Outdoors at any national park

SEVEN

How *Not* to Be the Date from Hell

Quick, choose up sides and don your raincoats, because when talk turns to the awful things men and women do to one another on dates, there is bound to be a whole heap of mudslinging. Few subjects inspire more vocal debate. Men forever defend themselves and claim to be maligned, misunderstood, and unfairly indicted for the dating crimes of a few bad apples. Meanwhile, women endlessly retell the countless tales of horror and legendary injustice forever foisted on them by thoughtless, cruel, insensitive guys! It's a wonder anyone ever goes out, considering how many horrendous first dates we've all suffered. Consider these choice examples:

Marni was stranded at a Manhattan night club during the worst blizzard in thirty years, thanks to a man who ran into an old girlfriend and, unbelievably, walked out with her, while Marni was waiting for him at the bar!

Fred had a first date with a woman who spent all of five minutes with him, and then canceled the date. Why? The lady in question apparently had Fred confused with another man she'd met recently who drove a Mercedes 500 convertible. When Fred walked her out to his beat-up 1986 Datsun, she decided to cut her losses!

And here's one for the record books. Leigh agreed to go out with an emergency room physician she met through a friend. She and the doctor arranged to meet at the hospital after his shift. When Leigh arrived, a nurse directed her to an office where the doctor was supposed to be. Leigh knocked several times on the slightly ajar door before nudging it open to see if her date was there. He was there all right. Or just about there actually, his pants bunched around his ankles, vigorously having sex with a nurse on top of his desk!

Was Leigh miffed? Oh, yes. Was her outrage justified? You bet. Most dating injuries and injustices are mild by comparison—and quite often, purely accidental.

Richie, a sales rep from Philadelphia, met Ann, who worked for the phone company, at a popular Society Hill bar. They hit it off immediately and got so wrapped up in chatting that the next thing they knew it was closing time. Convinced that she was the woman of his dreams, he got her phone number, slipped it into his jeans pocket, and promised to call in a day or two so they could arrange to meet for dinner on the weekend.

But the next day, while Richie was out of town on a sales trip, his well-intentioned but anal-retentive roommate decided to do Richie's laundry for him. When Richie returned home with

Ann on his mind, he went looking for her phone number only to find the bluejeans he'd worn the night before neatly folded along with his other clean clothes.

The only trace of Ann's number was an indecipherable blueish ball of pulp. Richie was horrified. Worse yet, since Ann's last name was a very common one and Richie had no idea which phone company she worked for, his chances of locating her were slim—although he did make a dozen calls trying to track her down. The last I heard, he was still hanging out at that same bar hoping and praying Ann would someday return.

There are lots of variables involved in making a positive first impression, going on a first date, and getting from that date into a new romance. Like the moving parts of an engine, everything has to be tuned up regularly and working perfectly for the machine to run well. And so many things can go wrong. You can be stood up simply because someone misplaced a phone number, or wrote down the wrong date, time or address. And whether by coincidence or misunderstanding or malicious intent, we all occasionally do things ourselves to thoroughly botch up a date.

Generally, after a man suffers a major dating disappointment, he'll gripe, growl, complain to his friends and then move on. We assume you do the same. But what if we conducted exit polls after every first date? What if we both knew what we had done right, and especially, what we had done wrong? Couldn't we stand to benefit knowing what makes one date memorable and another one "the date from hell!?"

First Impressions You Don't Want to Make

Greg, an Olympic-caliber athlete with a medal to prove it, drove over to the Seattle apartment building where he was due to pick up Pamela, a sports store manager he'd been fixed up with by a mutual friend. He parked his car, found the right apartment, and was about to ring the doorbell when Pamela's roommate June, who was about to leave for work, yanked opened the door. After they got over their initial surprise, Greg introduced himself and June invited him in. But before she could let Pamela know that her date had arrived, the bedroom door burst open and out came Pamela wearing nothing but her panties! The words "have you seen my . . ." barely escaped her lips before she noticed a handsome guy admiring her naked body. Now *that's* a first impression any guy is sure to remember (though it's probably not one you'd choose to make!). Blushing from head to toe, Pamela managed to do an about-face, find her clothes, and pull herself together in time to have a very fun and funny first date with Greg. However, not all flubbed first impressions lead to such happy endings.

On a cross-country flight, Will befriended a flight attendant named Denise, and they made a date for the following Friday night, when Denise would be in town for a few days. Keeping in mind that he had only seen her in a conservative skirt and regulation airlines blouse, you can imagine the look on Will's face when Denise, a leggy brunette, stepped out of the elevator into the lobby of her apartment building wearing a skin-tight miniskirt and sheer blouse with her lacy bra clearly visible beneath it. One look and Will knew that a movie and a burger probably weren't what she had in mind for their evening. So he swiftly changed his staid game plan, and took Denise to a funky downtown restaurant. Three daiquiris later, she suggested they go dancing. When the dance club closed at well after two in the morning, she invited Will up to her apartment. It won't come as a surprise to any guy that while Denise was waiting for the coffee to brew, Will put the moves on her, big time. Well, she stopped him cold and was annoyed as hell! *What kind of girl did he think she was?* Typical male answer? The kind of girl who wore tight minis and see-through blouses with lacy bras on first dates, and invited guys up to her apartment at 3 A.M., probably because she wanted to fool around.

While any halfway enlightened man will agree that Denise's provocative dress did *not* give Will carte blanche to expect any sexual favors, in this case most guys would stick up for him. He didn't *misread* the signals! If Denise didn't want to fool around on a first date, she was *sending* the wrong signals! She may not have intended to convey the message he received. Perhaps she dressed this same way whenever she was out of uniform. Or maybe drinking, dancing, and bringing men home to her apartment at 3 A.M. was her idea of good, clean fun.

But like most guys, Will would never guess that, and he responded the only way he knew how. Frustrated, he left without an argument, and didn't bother to call again.

This issue of what your clothes say can work both ways. Elizabeth, a California teacher, met a seemingly conservative fellow teacher at a seminar and agreed to go out to dinner with him. She dressed for the evening in chinos and a nice blouse with her hair pulled back in a bow. Her date showed up in leather shorts and a chain and leather vest with no shirt underneath. With the words "dangerous" and "disgusting" flashing like neon signs in her mind, Elizabeth didn't even open the door, much less go out with this guy.

As that old saying goes, "You never have a second chance to make a first impression." And your appearance—your looks, your hair, your clothes, the way you present yourself—is all men have to go on when they pick you up for a first date. Call it advertising if you will. You're sending out a message, which we'll interpret based on our knowledge and experience. Then we'll behave accordingly.

Although there is no way to predict how a particular man will respond to your appearance (a great first impression to some men may be a ticket out the door to others), there are some safe bets. Big hair, tons of makeup, pushup bras with low-cut dresses, spiked heels with miniskirts, and bare midriffs have a tendency to say, "I might want action." Natural hairstyles, the fresh-faced look, softly fitting dresses or blouses that leave details to the imagination, tailored skirts or slacks, all fall under headings like conservative and understated or stylish and subtly provocative. They're inviting enough to hold a man's interest but not so drop-dead sexy that he'll have trouble being interested in anything else about you. Of course, the look you choose never justifies rudeness or abuse. A date owes you proper courtesy even if you show up at the door dressed in a clown suit. However, your appearance most definitely will influence how you are viewed and treated by the men who go out with you. We don't often start out thinking that we'll end up in the sack on a first date, but if you're dressed for action, don't be utterly shocked if you get some. And if you're guilty of false advertising, don't be too surprised if a man goes home from a date unamused!

More First Date Faux Pas

The first time Tommy dated a young woman named Carol, they joined two other couples—his best friends—for dinner at a popular Maryland steak house. Everybody ordered beef, including Carol, who chose the filet mignon. When the waiter put her steak down in front of her, she turned to him and quite assertively announced, "I beg your pardon. I ordered the *filet* mignon. This isn't fish!" Ouch!

Dating is notorious for its embarrassing incidents and memorable moments like that one. Some are unpreventable and amusing. Others are well within a woman's control, and from the man's point of view, can fall under the category of our pet peeves. A prime example of this would be announcing that you have to be home at a certain hour right after we pick you up.

What does this do to the male psyche? Nothing very good. It sort of feels like Dad saying we have to have the car back by eleven. And it dashes any hopes we may have had for the evening to go wonderfully, spontaneously well. The skies won't open, and the seas won't part, and we won't be finding ourselves forever entangled in one another's hearts—if you announce you have to be home by 9:15! You might as well come right out and say, "I'm probably not going to like you. I doubt we're going to have any fun at all. And even if we do, you don't have a snowball's chance in hell of kissing me."

"Unfair," you cry. "Unreasonable!" What if you *do* have to be home at a certain time? Well, if it's for a good reason like a baby-sitter's curfew or to catch a flight, then we can handle it. But "I've got a lot of housework tomorrow so I have to be home by ten," or, "I'm really tired so I hope this is going to be an early night," definitely puts a damper on the evening. And nothing can compare to (or justify) the ultimate loser line: "My favorite show is on at nine. Do you think we'll be home by then?"

Some other pet peeves? Women who slather on makeup in our cars right after we pick them up. We don't get it. Would you like it if a guy pulled his electric razor out of the glovebox and grabbed a quick shave at a traffic light? If you're not ready when we arrive, just say so. We can wait. On the other hand, if the date is going well, a touch of lipstick between dinner and dancing is fine. Even kind of reassuring. If you're having enough fun to want to re-apply, it makes us feel special. Gives us the notion that maybe you like us.

Don't even *think* about telling us how to drive on a first date (unless you think your life is in jeopardy!). Don't suggest or insist that we stop and ask for directions to our destination. Please! You know how we are about this. Making or taking a call on your cellular flip phone (or worse yet, ours) is also very disconcerting. We hate feeling like second fiddle on a first date (or any date for that matter).

Smoking is a tricky issue because even though it is totally déclassé of late, about eight gazillion people still do it. All I can suggest is if you smoke and he doesn't, try not to light up immediately after you meet and every five minutes after that. A lot of men can handle an occasional puff, but chain-smoking strikes us as a nervous habit, and we don't like to think we make you *that* nervous. Ditto for nail biting. It's a real turnoff to watch you gnawing.

Yes, I know guys are guilty of all these same sins. And yes, we have some uniquely male habits that aggravate the heck out of you. Ogling other women. Drinking too much. Eating like animals. The list is long. I'm sure we match every one of your bothersome traits with three of our own. We hope you'll be as forgiving of our little peculiarities as we try to be about yours.

For both of us, these quirks can be easily ignored. You're nervous. We're nervous. Stuff happens. Seeking perfection is pointless. Demanding it on a first date is a prescription for disappointment. Moreover, for a man who has taken enough interest in you to ask you out, things like talking during the movie, ordering meals you don't eat, making silly puckering sounds as you apply your lipstick at the table, and other occasionally less-than-adorable tendencies are hardly deal-breakers. We can overlook all sorts of little habits (as we hope you can with us), if we both think our initial attraction is worth pursuing.

---

10 Things We Don't Want to Notice In Your Apartment

1. Cat hair on everything
2. Laundry basket full of really droopy, gray panties
3. Seductive pictures of you and your ex
4. TV blaring on the Home Shopping Network
5. Penicillin growing in your fridge next to the beer
6. Recently tossed condom wrappers
7. Photo of you and your father at a gun convention
8. Men's shaving kit in the bathroom
9. Mace
10. Your *new* Brad Pitt poster

DINNER DATE RIGOR MORTIS

There are a number of weighty issues that can really steer a date down the tubes, and one of them is dinner-table conversation. For instance, men have a bad habit of gabbing about their ex-girlfriends as a way to make small talk with a potential *new* girlfriend. There is a fairly simple way to get a man to stop. Tell him, "Hey, Gilbert, can we please talk about something else! I'm getting tired of hearing how horrible Angela was to you." It's blunt, to the point, and very effective.

When we're done blushing with shame, rest assured you'll hear no more about our old girlfriend.

What do *you* talk about over the chef's salad that drives *us* bonkers? Work, for starters, if you talk about it incessantly. Phillip, a marina manager, met Ruthanne, a buttoned-up accountant, at a charity benefit. They chatted over champagne and he invited her out to an artsy San Francisco bistro later in the week. At dinner, Phillip tried to wax poetic about music and art and travel, but all Ruthanne would talk about was her job. Now an accountant's job ranks high on the yawn scale to begin with, and two hours on the tax benefits of taking out a second mortgage is way too much in anyone's book. In Phillip's opinion, it sent a clear message. *She's not romantically interested in me.*

Was Phillip being super sensitive? Perhaps. But if you keep up a three-hour monologue about work, the mood of your date is going to be anything but intimate. Think about it. The lights are low. The wine is poured. The piano is playing quietly in the background. And you're talking about the latest predictions for the prime interest rate? How sexy is that?

Talking too much and too fast about absolutely nothing also drives men crazy (and not in a good way)! Perhaps you do it out of nervousness. Or in your defense, perhaps your date is not the most scintillating conversationalist, so you're filling dead air. But let's assume he is attractive and intelligent and capable of stringing together a couple of three-syllable words in a row. Why would you insist on conducting a 78-rpm monologue on your boss's toupee? And why do women seem to launch into these mini-lectures right after we've said something serious that reveals our feelings about her?

Perhaps you recognize the moment. It usually hits after that first cocktail. We've just finished telling you about a fish we caught in Bimini or a business trip that took us to Kuala Lumpur, and there's a lull in the conversation. That's when something comes over us. We look up at you and suddenly we're in love! We spot the light in your eyes or the way your hair falls over your shoulders or the subtle crook of your smile, and something clicks. We feel compelled to halt everything and tell you how glad we are to be there with you. We're hoping to elicit a wonderful, meaningful comment from you. But what do we occasionally get in return?

The second you see that mentally carnivorous look in our eye—you start babbling! Or that's what it sounds like to us, anyway. Here's an example. We're having a really great time and we want you to know, so we say: "Gee Veronica. I am so glad I met you!" From the look on your face, one would think we had just mooned the maître d'. You recover with words. "Oh. Well, uhhh, thanks Patrick. Say! Did I tell you about the time my friend's Mom won a basket-weaving competition in South America? She picked her own bamboo. Which reminds me of the summer we spent at the beach in Brazil. Well it wasn't actually a summer. Just three weeks when my Dad was in the foreign service. Only I didn't like it much because I couldn't speak Portuguese. . . ."

If our occasional crime is overenthusiasm, yours is this kind of defensive conversationalism.

We both are going to babble a little bit on our early dates. But when a man takes you out, he not only finds you drop-dead gorgeous, he's also hoping to come away with some sense of who you are. We don't expect you to recite Neruda or rhapsodize about the possibility of our someday swimming naked together in a Caribbean cay. But if you feel any chemistry at all, open up a smidgen. Share some intimate piece of knowledge. Tell us about your favorite childhood memory. Or how you cook gourmet meals for yourself even if you're eating alone. Or how you like to listen to Brahms in the tub. It give us something to take home in our minds. Otherwise we're not going to know if we've been on a date or a job interview!

We'd rather you got a little too personal or shared one story you shouldn't have, rather than diligently making small talk for four hours and sending us home without a clue as to what you are like. We need something to hook into if we're going to ask you out on another date, and rumor has it that you want that "something" to include your mind and personality, as well as our initial attraction to your looks.

Topics You Should Avoid Discussing Over Dinner

- Dieting
- Your ex-boyfriend's band
- Gum surgery
- Your roommate's foot problems
- Your boss who keeps hitting on you

Topics You Wish *We'd* Avoid Discussing Over Dinner

- Our ex (the Olympic volleyball player)
- Any movies starring Demi Moore
- Graphic descriptions of our knee surgery
- Our mother—for more than ten minutes
- Our boss who keeps hitting on us

MORE OF OUR LEAST FAVORITE THINGS

David did not like country music. He certainly had no interest in line dancing. But his date, Terry, kept insisting that he'd love it if he just gave it a try. *Open-mindedness is good,* he thought. *Compromise is the key to a successful relationship.* So he agreed to go to Terry's favorite country-and-western bar. He tried line dancing and was awful at it. But he didn't have to worry about making a fool of himself in front of Terry. She was too busy two-stepping with a cowboy she met during an earlier line dance to even notice when David left the club after fifteen minutes of watching her have a great time with someone other than him.

There are few things more hurtful or offensive than having your date run off with someone else. While it can be an awful blow to either gender, to a guy it seems a double whammy. After going out on a limb to ask you out, he not only strikes out, but has to watch some other guy succeed where he failed!

What are some other first-date blunders that make men wonder why they ever asked you out in the first place? Spending the entire evening worrying about how you look. We asked you out. Obviously we think you are attractive. Having an entire asparagus spear lodged in your teeth might be just cause to make a beeline to the bathroom. But it's really tiresome to have you running off every ten minutes to fix your makeup, or to listen to you fretting about your looks all evening. We don't care! We love the way you look. Remember—we asked you out! Stop fixing what ain't broke!

Cataloguing what you're looking for (or not looking for) in a guy ten minutes after your date picks you up is not especially endearing or entertaining. *"I can't stand men who expect me to sleep with them on a first date,"* you proclaim over appetizers. Thanks for sharing that kernel of truth, we think. We never knew! Or, *"This guy I went out with last week made me split the dinner bill. Can you believe it?"* Okay. We get the hint! And how about this: *"I'm definitely not up for getting involved with anyone."* Gee whiz, that's terrific. Remind us again—why are we out on this date?

Granted, we ask you out because we want to know more about you. And we don't want to edit your comments, or ever limit you from telling a great or amusing story. But we don't need to hear every single one of your complaints (any more than you want to hear all of ours). We're sorry that some members of the male gender are so deviant. And we're sorry you've been mistreated by other men. We know that guys can be real creeps on a date. But those are other guys—not us. And there's not much we can do about the past, and we were sort of hoping to be a bright part of your future. We just need you to give us a chance.

As long as we're coming clean, here are a few other crimes and misdemeanors. *Wearing too much perfume.* If our car windows start to fog, you've probably overapplied. *Arguing about who pays for dinner.* We don't mind if you want to split the check or pick up an after-dinner drink, but please don't start World War III over pitching in your share. Your generous offer is appreciated. You can even put a twenty on the table and gently insist. But if your date firmly (and kindly) says this is his treat, just thank him and enjoy. Or tell him *you* have the next round. That's a gesture most guys understand. *Looking at your watch every twenty minutes.* Are you meeting Tom Hanks for a nightcap or are we just that dull?! And a very common turnoff? *Going to check your message machine* (unless there is a real emergency which you have to monitor). How would you feel if we left you sitting by yourself while we called Sports Phone for those urgent, up-to-the-minute baseball scores!

As I check off these little habits that annoy men, you'll no doubt notice that plenty of them are things that we do that annoy you, too! There's probably a lesson for both of us to learn here. The only way two near strangers can find common ground and enjoy each other's company is if they both behave reasonably, and treat one another with respect.

SEX AND THE EX

Want to test a guy's sexual mettle? Try this. When you're making love with him for the first time and he asks, "Does that feel good?" you reply: "It's okay. I think my last boyfriend must have been bigger." You might as well rig a bucket of ice water over your bed and keep the draw cord nearby. An icy shower would have the same effect.

It's not that we're jealous of your past lovers. We rather boldly assume that there isn't a chance they could be as skilled as we are. But we just aren't interested in the details. We don't want to watch videotapes of how your last boyfriend performed oral sex. We don't want to make love with a stopwatch running to see who lasted longer. And it doesn't do us any good to know whether your orgasms with Mister Ex were twos or tens on the Richter scale. We can't be him, and we don't want to use *his* little tricks to drive you crazy. We have our own style and we want our lovemaking with you to feel fresh, new, and completely original.

Of course, when you're first starting out with a new lover, there is a natural tendency to compare. We do it too. And we know you'd be hurt if we told you how you measured up to our previous lovers. So please, we implore you, save the comparisons for your girlfriends (the same as we do with the guys). If you make us feel like we can't satisfy you the way the last guy did, we probably won't try very hard (or stick around) for very long.

What else makes guys cringe when they're first going to bed with you? A lot of men are turned off by sexually goal-oriented women. It kills the romance and spontaneity of our seductions. There's no element of surprise. Especially when we're first getting intimate, we like to view you as a blank canvas and we'll break down walls and start wars to get the opportunity to make an impression—hopefully a great one. But if we're being subtly pressured to perform, we're likely to wonder, "Where's the fun?"

We can definitely live without the sexual-drill-sergeant routine, especially when we're just starting out. "Do this. Do that. Don't stop. One-two, one-two, faster, harder, one-two!" We hope we know how to make love to a woman. We can usually tell what you like and are quick to respond to the telltale clues your body gives us. A little graphic bedroom dialogue and a few meaningful groans are fine too. We don't mind the murmured, "Ooooh, that feels nice. Right there. Keep doing *that!*" But no man likes a woman who barks orders during lovemaking. It's one thing to help us out and coax us along as we're seducing or making love to you. It's another when you grab a guy's head and nearly break his neck trying to twist it into some physically impossible anatomical position, while you're counting out tongue cadences as you crack a whip!

Orgasm counters aren't our favorite lovemaking partners, either. Let's say we've been on your couch for an hour, voraciously necking and fondling and stroking you while you've been working us into a frenzy with your loving attentions. We scramble into the bedroom and tear off each other's remaining clothes. Then, being typical guys with big egos, we perform every act known to animalkind on you. We do this because we love pleasing you. Your orgasm(s) are a source of tremendous pride for us.

After we work each other into a sweat-covered frenzy, you finally retrieve a condom from your bedside table and we make love to you for as long and with as much passion as we can muster (if it's the first time, guys will silently recite the entire elements chart or complicated algebra problems just to stave off ejaculation a few seconds longer). Finally, when we can't stand it any more, we climax. Simultaneously maybe. Or maybe it's your third orgasm of the evening.

However, since it is our first time together, you may have had fun but not reached orgasm. No matter how much we'd like to jump right back into the fray to ultimately please you, men tend to need time out following such a monumental lovemaking session. We collapse, fall asleep for a bit. It's a biological necessity. One habit that often makes us a bit crazy is when you coyly roll over on top of us right then and say, "Is that all?" Or reach for our member and try to resuscitate him three minutes after we've finished (and probably as we're starting to snore). Whether your overture is oral or manual, chances are it's unwelcome at that particular moment. Do you think we'd be falling into a drooling sleep if we were physically up for an encore performance? Of course not! Unless you're dating a 16-year-old, you'll have to give it a rest until our batteries are recharged.

First-time sex can be fairly stressful for a guy. Of course we want you to be multi-orgasmic. We want you to love our every sensuous, impassioned exploration of your body. But we want it to be a shared journey. Would you give a guy the time of day if all he cared about was coming and going? Well, if you're measuring your lovers by quantity instead of quality, you'll find that they tend to vanish quickly as well.

A Few Bedroom Dos and Don'ts

DON'T	DO
Cross your arms and say "Is that all?" if you didn't quite get there before he did.	Gently slow him down and show him exactly what you like. He will be delighted to oblige.
Throw him out before dawn just because your apartment's a mess.	Throw him out before dawn because your Mom's coming over!
Even think about having sex without a condom.	Keep a box of fresh condoms by your bedside just in case!

THE DREADED CORNER

Matt, a 32-year-old perpetual bachelor and lady's man, was dating Linda, a woman he worked with who was a couple of years older than he was. And for once in his life, Matt did not try to rush into bed after a couple of dinners out. Two months passed before they made love for the first time at a romantic inn on the New Jersey shore. The sex turned out to be exciting and comfortable and nice, and they spent most of the rest of that weekend in bed exploring their new sexual relationship. For Matt's nickel, this pleasant turn of events was great. That was until Monday morning.

That was when Linda, who had already decided she was Matt's steady girl, proceeded to let everyone in their office know that they were an item. Before Matt had even enjoyed a few days of accepting his newfound feelings toward Linda, she was engaging in physical displays of affection at the office. She started e-mailing him and calling several times a day, and basically assuming that they were into this new affair for the long run. Now Matt may have had strong feelings for Linda. He certainly demonstrated that on their first weekend, in private. But men can be a bit slow at times about taking their feelings out on the street. As a result, Matt felt blindsided by Linda's assumption that their romance was now a matter of public record.

A man who has actively dated around for the past five years needs a little time to get used to the idea of having a steady girlfriend. While Matt did not necessarily want to keep sleeping around and dating every female who walked, things were happening way too quickly. He needed to gradually ease into what had begun as a slow romance. He needed time for his heart to assuage the fears of commitment that he had been acting on for years. But he found himself backed into the corner instead. What exactly is this dreaded corner men seem to fear?

It is the place guys feel women try to get us to when we're just beginning a new relationship. Our reluctance to get "involved" is *not* necessarily a symptom of commitment-phobia. Men who try to get out of a relationship after just a few weeks by claiming, "I'm not into commitment," are lying! It's an excuse we fabricate to escape from the corner we believe you have painted us into by altering your larger view of our budding romance, once we've had sex for the first time.

The transformation can occur from fifteen minutes to eight hours after intercourse, and definitely involves more than the passing awkwardness that strikes most couples the morning after. Men and women both get excited when we first "do it." Our emotions get jumbled up and confused. But more often than not, once we have a chance to catch our breath, we settle down. Now guys know that the *tone* of our dealings with you are supposed to change afterwards. We're *supposed* to feel a difference once we've done something as intimate as lovemaking. But does that mean our relationship has to change instantly, or completely, the very next day?

When a man gets home after a night of lovemaking, he will definitely look forward to seeing you again really soon. We want to pursue our relationship with you further, but on a more even keel. We're looking for a steady glow rather than a runaway roller-coaster ride. In other words, we *are* capable of settling down, but it sometimes takes us a little time to get used to the idea of retiring our "singlehood" number. We're not asking you to let us prowl the bars and beaches looking for 18-year-old cheerleaders to practice our wiles on while we consider whether you are the woman for us. But we do need you to let us ease slowly into a new relationship.

We need time to step back and think about the ways being lovers will change our romance. We need our space, which doesn't necessarily mean we want out. Quite often all we're saying is that we want to go slowly and carefully and let things develop on all fronts—sexual and emotional—one step at a time. If we're meant to be with you, we'll figure it out soon enough. Matt might have figured that out about Linda in time, but time was precisely what she did not give him.

Guys tend to run from pushy women. We also run from dates who demand too much too early, and while we're discussing this—we're not real good with ultimatums either. So what *does* work? How do you nudge the man teetering on the verge of romance into a more steady relationship?

Flowers work wonders. Especially for no reason. A gentle invite to a romantic dinner at your place. Great sex when we least expect it. A sweet phone message after a really nice evening. And sometimes limiting physical contact to only a long kiss and a warm hug at the end of a date—especially after we've started sleeping together. (Just because we've made love once doesn't mean we have to do it every time.) If we've dated you and waited patiently to make love to you, then the odds are we have an eye on a more serious relationship. At times though, we need you to humor us for a while—not forever, but at least a few more dates with you—until we get used to the idea.

Learning to Laugh

Kurt, a gentlemanly Cleveland businessman out on a date, didn't realize that the restaurant he had chosen for a romantic dinner had a "cash only" policy until he tried to pay the bill with his credit card. He raced to the nearest automatic teller machine, and due to a computer foul-up, repeatedly received a "No Available Balance" message—and of course, no money. As a result, he had no choice but to ask his date to loan him the money to pay for their meal.

The next day an embarrassed and apologetic Kurt brought flowers to this woman's office along with the hundred bucks she had shelled out the night before. But the trouble he'd gone to, and the sincerity of his gesture, were lost on her. She handed him back the flowers and told him never to call her again.

It is insensitive, inflexible actions like this woman's that prompt guys to utter the three words women always hate to hear—"What a bitch!"—although in this case, our women friends might use the same label. And if a guy behaved similarly, they'd no doubt employ the counterpart line: "What an ass****!"

There are certain things you can do to absolutely guarantee a man will never call you back again. For example: *Make him feel rotten about money if he's trying his hardest to be generous.* Works like a charm. (And makes us wonder: if you're so wise and independent, how come you're not offering to chip in?) *Criticize his car—and I don't mean as a joke.* Do you think we want to drive a 1976 wreck? We promise that's not by choice. Do you want to date us, or our wheels? *Laugh at him in bed when he's trying his hardest to please you.* Herein lies the great dividing line that separates a potential girlfriend from a one-night stand. If the lovemaking or foreplay isn't quite monumental the first or second time, the woman who criticizes or angrily rolls over, or worse, storms out, will end up a notch in our bedboard. (And we will talk about her mercilessly to every one of our friends.) On the other hand, the woman who can laugh *with* us about our performance or hers, or *anything* we do in bed, is the one we'll stick by.

A sense of humor is the key to any good, lasting relationship—or any decent date, for that matter. The fact is, awful things that are completely out of our control have been known to occur while we're out on a date with you. Pete and Katy, two college students, were driving home from a wonderful day: eight hours at an outdoor folk festival in northern Georgia. As Katy slept, Pete, who was thinking about how happy he was with his new girlfriend, smiled broadly, and that smile remained plastered to his face right up until he noticed a police car's flashing red beacon in his rearview mirror. Katy awoke as Pete pulled his car to the shoulder. She patted him reassuringly on the thigh as if to say, "It's okay. It happens to all of us." And normally getting a speeding ticket really *is* no reason to get bent out of shape. But what Katy didn't know and Pete *did* was that he had received three tickets over the past two years. (Bad luck. Sharp radar. Bored traffic cop.) And what's worse, he couldn't remember whether he had paid them all. As the trooper took Pete's license back to the car to run a check, Pete prayed that the computers would be down. An hour later, he prayed that the rambunctious drunk in his jail cell would pass out soon and remain asleep for the rest of the night.

Getting busted on a date would make it onto most women's "Greatest Dating Bloopers" video, but Katy liked Pete and already knew he had a reckless side. In fact, everyone in Pete's fraternity was known to be a little "heavy on the pedal." So while Pete languished in his Georgia jail cell, Katy called three of his frat brothers and convinced them to scrape up bail and make a hundred-mile road trip in the middle of the night. Three hours later, as the sun came up over Interstate 75, Katy, Pete, and his friends were enjoying a hearty breakfast at a roadside truck stop. Call it a happy ending to what could have been a disastrous date—and a clear-cut example of the kind of woman most men love, a woman who knows how to roll with the punches.

Awful things that are completely out of our control often happen when we go out with you. Thanks to the bad oysters that began our meal, we end our evening in the local emergency room. The cozy country inn we saw advertised in a travel brochure turns out to be a lot less cozy than it looked. Or your date's car breaks down—which happens more often than any guy wants to think about. (One man was driving on the interstate when his date spotted a tire bounding down an embankment alongside their car. He can still recall the look of horror on her face when she realized it was his!) How well you deal with these little indignities deeply colors our feelings about you.

If we both lighten up and simply look at a date as a chance to get to know one another, then our ability to have a good time can increase a hundredfold. Much better to kiss goodnight and go home laughing, than crying, any night of the week.

10 Things Guys Admit They Have Very Little Sense of Humor About

1. Their cars
2. Other guys' nicer cars
3. Lack of cash
4. Sub-five-minute climaxes
5. Handsome waiters who know more than they do
6. Overcooking dinner for you
7. Rejected credit cards
8. Bumping into your old boyfriend
9. Your not minding bumping into your old boyfriend
10. Your getting angry when we take a *swing* at your old boyfriend

EIGHT

From Date to Boyfriend

Jim attended a small New England college. So small, as a matter of fact, that women from a nearby women's college used to journey there by bus to round out their social mixers and parties. At one such gathering, Jim met one of these college girls whom I'll call Sally. Jim and Sally drank and danced and laughed at the party. Then they drank and danced and laughed some more in Jim's dorm room, which was where they were when Sally's college bus loaded up and left without her. Stranded, with no place to stay but with Jim, Sally insisted that "she never did stuff like this." She mentioned that several more times that night as she and Jim had sex twice (and attempted a third time) before finally collapsing, totally spent, at dawn.

A few hours later, as Jim lay in bed nursing a hangover, young Sally calmly plucked a toothbrush and clean panties from her handbag and hightailed it to the dorm bathroom to clean up. *How curious,* Jim thought, *for someone who "never did stuff like that" to be traveling with tooth-*

brush and panties in her purse! Later that morning, Jim drove Sally back to her college, bought her a cup of coffee at the student union building, and half-heartedly promising to call, limped back to his home turf. Not surprisingly that was Jim's first and last date with Sally.

I don't know too many guys who would pass judgment on Sally. More likely, most would be kicking themselves for not dancing with her first. And I wouldn't criticize any grownup today who knew about safe sex, used a condom, and made a mutual decision with another adult to have sex on a crazy all-night first date. Of course, there's about a one-in-a-hundred chance that one of those wild romps will develop into a lasting romance. More often than not, they end the next morning in slightly embarrassed silence or sparse, shallow conversation over a quick cup of coffee, and then a dual sigh of relief, a quick farewell, and a return to their separate lives.

One-night stands serve their purpose. They let two people with a need or desire have their fun—and then go their own ways. These occasional, virtually anonymous trysts are nothing more than a breaking of convention. And conventional wisdom tells us sleeping around is not the way to win a lasting mate—boyfriend or girlfriend.

Despite every man's desire to be thought of as reckless, spontaneous and unconventional, in actuality we are quite predictable. When it comes to forging a meaningful relationship, there are certain patterns we seem to follow and certain signs we look for. That is not to say that men hold every date up to a yardstick and dump her if she doesn't measure up. But just as you can tell a fun-loving frat rat from a serious boyfriend-type in a Budweiser second, we know which girls we meet are for fun and which are for real. And just as you can distinguish "boy-toys" from "husband material" based on our behavior on early dates, we have found that there are certain things *you* do—certain behaviors and certain reassurances you give us—that influence whether we view you as "date" material or "girlfriend" material.

After we've been out on a few dates with you, we can see our romance begin to take shape. We start to notice changes, mood swings, ups and downs. If we're having a great time most of the time, those will just be speed bumps along the way to a more enduring affair. Are there ways to help us get there a bit more quickly? Things you can do to nudge us toward a relationship? Or clues that the cute guy you're dating is ready to become the boyfriend you take home to Mom?

IF YOU'RE INTERESTED, LET HIM KNOW

Walter went on a first date with Maura, had a great time, and not only called her, but sent flowers to work the next day. Maura never went out with him again. Meanwhile, Gerry, a serious lady-killer, never called his dates back until an hour before he wanted to go out with them. Yet women waited on the edge of their seats for his calls, and went out with him again and again. Go figure.

When *should* a man call after a first date, then?

The next morning? A day later? A week or two? We beg your indulgence if we had a great time and call too soon (like a half hour after we've kissed you goodnight at your door). Clearly, we like you. We know all the rulebooks say we're supposed to play a little hard to get, but if it's truly a fantastic date we can't help but show a little enthusiasm. And we wouldn't mind if you did the same. There's nothing so sexy and reassuring to a man as a message on his machine when he gets home from a date with you. "Hi Biff. It's Jennie. Thanks for the really nice dinner. Don't worry about the wine stains—I think they're going to come out. And by the way, I really had a great time. Don't call back tonight. I'm going to bed now. G'night!" We love this! It makes us feel good about the date. It gives us confidence to call you back and ask you out again really soon. Best of all, we get to hear your bedroom voice and picture you climbing under the sheets and wonder what you're wearing. These are all very good things!

After we've been on a few dates and there is definitely a mutual attraction, the timing of phone calls takes on additional meaning. When the purpose of the call is to set up a date, men tend to operate on a somewhat standard schedule. Nothing ever happens more than a week ahead of time (unless we have an incredibly busy business schedule that requires real advance planning). For a weeknight date, we'll call on a Monday morning. It makes our plan part of the work week's activity. A Friday night date? That's a rather casual invite and we might not pick up the phone until midweek. A Saturday night date is a pretty big deal, so we'll try to tie that one down almost a week in advance. (The logic is that on a Friday night if you have other plans, we'll go out with our buddies, but on a Saturday night we want to be sure we're going to see you—and perhaps be sure you're not out with someone else!) Of course, these aren't hard, fast rules; they are merely a window to our thinking. What's more, our ultimate goal is not to have to use the phone for date scheduling at all. We'll both know that casual dating has turned into a comfortable romance when it's more or less assumed that we're going to be doing *something* together on the weekend.

As you might expect, men will respond emotionally if you turn down enough of their invites. If you're never available for a casual weekday date, for example, men feel tons of pressure to make the weekend date special. Thinking "this is my big chance," a guy will go all out to give you the red carpet treatment, when you might just be up for a movie and a salad. This is a situation ripe for misunderstanding.

Needing a month's notice to go out with us on a Saturday night won't work in your favor, either. It gets us wondering about why you aren't available. Is it because you have a boyfriend? Is your calendar so full of dates that we just don't rank? Or are you feeling lukewarm toward us and not willing to commit to a Saturday night? You may have a half-dozen perfectly good excuses for turning down a month of Saturday invites. (Maybe you're a member of the space shuttle crew on a mission. Or you just won the Nobel prize in physics and have to be in Stockholm to accept.) But we have limited patience when waiting for a serious date. Reject a man enough, and he'll be off to greener pastures in no time.

THE DATES THAT RAISE THE STAKES

Love can bloom in many places. A crowded bar. A best friend's wedding. An all-night coffee shop. Or in the bleachers at Cleveland's Jacobs Field.

Sam, a Cleveland mechanic and ardent baseball fan, was dating Elizabeth, an office manager he met at a friend's party. Their dates thus far had been perfectly adequate, traditional fare. Action movie and pasta. Artsy movie and Indian food. And a casual, last minute, let's-grab-a-burger-after-work date. (That's the one where we first try to make the tone of our budding relationship a bit more informal. When you say "yes" to a casual, off-the-cuff invite, it immediately moves us a notch closer to a relationship.)

The true breakthrough for Sam and Elizabeth came at the end of a long, cold, miserable Cleveland winter that had stretched well into spring. Like all diehard baseball fans, by late March Sam's mind had turned to opening day—which he would have loved to attend. However, tickets for the Cleveland Indians' home opener at "the Jake," as Jacobs Field is known to locals, were impossible to get. Or almost impossible, as it turned out, since Sam got a call on game day from a customer who had two tickets to the 1 P.M. game and an emergency to deal with. Could Sam use the tickets, he wanted to know?

Dumb question. Men feign angina pains or quit jobs for opening day seats, and Sam was no exception. When he asked himself whom he could call at 10 A.M. on a midweek workday to take with him, Elizabeth immediately came to mind. But he worried, was going to a ballgame too "boylike" an activity? Did he know her well enough to call on twenty minutes notice? Would she even consider taking time off to go to opening day at The Jake?

Sam took the risk and dialed Elizabeth, who turned out to be totally cool about coming up with an excuse to skip out of work and play hooky with a man she was just getting to know. As a result, she was there at the Jake with the spring sunshine basking down on her and Sam (and fifty thousand exuberant fans), when a dramatic hit caused the stadium to erupt into a celebration. It also happened to lead to their first really passionate kiss.

Romance bloomed on the merit of that one date. In Sam's mind, the others had all been nice, but merely lukewarm, explorations. However, their stolen afternoon at the ballpark set Elizabeth apart from all the other women that had recently passed through his life without inspiring him to dive into a real, lasting romance.

Like Sam and Elizabeth's, most first date venues tend to run the traditional route. Dinner, a movie, an after-dinner cocktail. We go to these places to test the waters. We choose them because they're safe and easy and fairly predictable, giving us both an opportunity to get better acquainted without the stress of dealing with unfamiliar activities or locations. Granted, things can go wrong in even the most mundane of settings. But for the most part we like the comfort zone that a "standard" first date provides and we'll often stick with it for a while. A month will go by and we'll have seen three movies. We'll know you like cashew chicken and wonton soup. We'll have a pretty good idea of how you dress and what radio station you listen to and what you like to do with your weekends.

After we've played our opening hand and you've played yours, the game gets a little more interesting. Dating you becomes more of a challenge. We have to provide a little spin on the routine and you have to let us know how interested you are. Have we registered on your curiosity scale? Are you feeling something a little special toward us? Have we become a gossip item with your friends and workmates yet? We're also wondering how many other guys you're still dating and what we have to do to set ourselves ahead of the pack.

When we ask you out on a seemingly casual date, chances are we have a lot more than the *venue* on our mind. If the guy you've been dating for a while asks you to the zoo, it's probably not because he has a burning desire to hang out in the snake house. Hiking to a mountaintop usually suggests a lot more than a good view. A trip to a museum offers opportunities beyond art appreciation. We pick these places hoping that they'll have some special appeal to you. We're trying to stand out; to make our relationship with you feel unique, and to move it to a more personal level.

Go on these more creative dates with an open mind. It's our way of saying we like you and want to explore this romance further. Better yet, if you're dating a man who hasn't stepped off the straight and narrow yet, take the initiative yourself. Do you sense he spends every Sunday sucked into the impression on his couch with the remote control adhered to his palm? Invite him to a classical music concert. It's hard to say no to an event that you bought tickets for (except during any sport's playoff season or on the day of a huge game. Best not to try it then.). Some other possibilities? A San Diego woman took a man out for a half-day catamaran sail on Mission Bay. A Kansas City businesswoman with a brand-new convertible took her beau on a drive through the scenic Flint Hills of Kansas. A Bangor, Maine woman dating a carpenter led him by the hand to a summer blueberry picking festival. These are things lots of guys might not do by themselves. But we'll generally leap at the opportunity if the woman we're dating makes the suggestion. It spices up our courtship, and if you're the instigator, it sends us a strong message that you're really interested in us.

---

10 Great Places for a First Kiss

1. Floor seats at an NBA game
2. The beach just after sunset
3. A drive-in movie theater
4. Central Park during a summer outdoor concert
5. San Francisco anytime!
6. A picnic
7. Top of a London double-decker bus
8. Front seat of an old car with a bench seat
9. Fourth of July rodeo
10. Your front porch on a hot summer's night

THE SEDUCTION DANCE

Sometimes men and women cross the threshold from date to lover in a hail of glory. A bold young woman, Tara, quite astonishingly admits to being so turned on by a man she'd been dating that after they'd been out on five dates without any major action, she actually seduced him in a movie theater where they wound up making love in the back row of the balcony. Guys hear stories of young lust in the last car of an empty subway, in the fire stairwell of a high-rise apartment building, and on every beach from Miami to the rocky coast of Maine.

If a man is excited and you're willing, a six-foot snow bank won't dampen his enthusiasm. Remarkably enough, parked cars are still a veritable hotspot for sexual foreplay. Consider it a tribute to our past (or to movies from the fifties). If we find ourselves sitting in a car with you for more than three minutes, we simply have to try to touch your breast. You could be spilling top government secrets as we sit in front of your home and all we'd hear is the blood racing in our skulls. We must make a move or we're going to explode. But not every spark ignites an *instant* tryst, which is just fine with us. A slow, sultry seduction can be just as much fun as a wild, headlong dash to the bed. Men like slow. We love provocative. There's little that's more exciting than undressing you with our eyes before we undress you bit by bit with our trembling hands. Ditto for you undressing us.

Theo, a jazz aficionado, relied heavily on a special tape to measure the evening's progress. It had one especially soulful, sexy, fifteen minute saxophone track programmed about twenty-five minutes into it. And whenever Theo got a woman back to his apartment, after he brewed the coffee or opened a bottle of wine, he would pop in "the moves tape." He'd try to start making out by the time the sax track came on, and if he wasn't touching some portion of naked skin by its conclusion, he knew he probably wasn't going to have a big night. While all guys certainly aren't that deliberate, most of us do plan for lovemaking. We try to come up with the best possible time, place, and ambiance, and we suspect you do too.

Wendy, a fashion designer in New York, had been dating Ethan, a handsome, brilliant, and very reserved book editor. They'd worked the New York literary circle, going to all the coolest parties and readings and bookworm bars in Manhattan. They hit it off intellectually, but much to Wendy's dismay, ol' Ethan was taking his sweet time getting physical. Except for a few lingering kisses at her apartment door, he hadn't made a single untoward move. So rather than leaving their sex life to fate, Wendy decided to turn up the heat.

On a snowy Saturday afternoon after coming out of a foreign film, Wendy offered to cook Ethan dinner at her place instead of going out to yet another trendy bistro. Rather surprised (but not unpleasantly), he accepted. Wendy led Ethan through several of New York's finest markets, plotting the meal as she picked through exotic mushrooms, imported tomatoes, designer lettuces, and fresh pastas. Then she allowed Ethan to slip away and shop for a bottle of good red wine while she ran upstairs to quickly straighten her apartment.

Ethan returned with the wine, in no way prepared for the turn of events that would follow. He gamely played assistant to Wendy's chef. Cooking together is a warm and cozy and intimate activity under most circumstances. Cooking together in a tiny New York kitchen is down and outright lascivious. Bodies tend to rub together in all the right places while trying to wash lettuce and chop onions and sauté garlic in a space large enough for a toaster. Three glasses of wine before dinner never hurts either. By the time Wendy and Ethan had the meal ready, the kitchen windows were steamed over from the heat, their shoes were off, shirts untucked, and they both looked like they'd just prepared a feast for twenty. They quickly set a table, served dinner, toasted their good luck—and kissed. (I hear the food reheated quite nicely after they spent the next two hours exploring each others' bodies.)

If you've been dating a man for weeks or even months and he hasn't done more than lay a wimpy kiss or two on you, Wendy's recipe for romance might be just what you need. The fact that a guy hasn't seduced you doesn't automatically mean that he isn't interested. Perhaps he is shy. Or he's been burned recently and is unsure of himself. If you've been dating him for a good long while, though, and you're feeling pretty positive about the relationship even though no sparks have flown yet, why not go out on a limb and take matters into your own hands?

Whether we finally bring you up to our place or you initiate the first moves at yours, the effect is the same. We both cross a threshold from casual dating to the beginning of a sexual affair that announces our passion and trust for one another. It smoothes the way to all the pleasures we associate with foreplay and making love. And it signals the beginning of a romance that might have legs.

If he hasn't made his move yet, try . . .

1. Slow dancing with him after dinner at your place. You lead, one suggestive step at a time.
2. A deluxe backrub. Take his shirt off, spare no muscles, and don't forget his chest and butt. He'll either be aroused (or relaxedly asleep) in no time.
3. Leaving your bra at home one night. Go out in a tee. Don't ask why, but it drives men wild!
4. Inviting him to your parents' beach house or cabin when they're not using it. Get the fireplace going, break out the champagne, put on the soft music and light candles. He'll get the picture.
5. A day hike to a remote location. You'll both get hot and sweaty. Consider stopping to sunbathe (wearing as little as possible), or suggest skinny-dipping if there is a convenient (and secluded) lake or quarry pool.

PLANNING A LOST WEEKEND

San Francisco. Crisp ocean breezes, brilliant blue skies. Steep streets plunging to the bay, cable cars rattling by. Golden Gate Bridge in the distance. This was where Doug, a California dentist, was when he realized he was truly in love (not just "like") with his new girlfriend Carol. Their first weekend date was in a romantic room with a bay view at a fancy Nob Hill hotel. They checked in. Made love. Rode the cable car to Pier 39. Took silly tourist pictures. Ate dungeness crab sandwiches. Bought chocolate at Ghiradelli Square. Hiked back to the hotel. After sunset cocktails and before dinner in Chinatown, they made love again. Then they listened to jazz in North Beach and wound down at the piano bar in their hotel. Doug and Carol fell asleep to the twinkling lights of the sparkling San Francisco skyline, and woke up together the next morning in a beautiful suite where they shared a sexy bath and made love, *again.* You get the picture.

A weekend date can mean many different things to a new relationship. It can be as grandiose as a first-time lover sweeping you away to Paris for cafés and "vin rouge" and strolls along the Seine, before making love to you in a romantic, old hotel as the spring sunlight glows over the Louvre. Or it can be as down-to-earth as waking up for the first time together on a Sunday morning, and jointly destroying the kitchen while making pancakes and bacon. Either way, the long weekend date is everything a man has aspired to from the moment he first laid eyes on you.

Martin, who lived in suburban Virginia had been dating Charlotte, a Washington lobbyist, for several months. Their first time lovemaking unfolded in Charlotte's Georgetown apartment on a

Friday night and ended wrapped in one another's arms on Saturday morning. Martin politely mumbled, "maybe I should go," but Charlotte silenced his meek offer by making love to him again. When he awoke three hours later, she had rounded up a newspaper and made him a fantastic brunch. By then, it was the middle of the afternoon, and it had started to rain, so they took in a new exhibit at a local museum, and then a movie. After the movie, they had a bite to eat at a cozy cafe. Then the next thing they knew, they were back in bed. Martin didn't actually head back to Virginia until late Sunday afternoon!

Our favorite way to spend a first weekend with you is right at home: yours or ours. This is especially wonderful if it's as unplanned and spontaneous as Martin and Charlotte's weekend was. Why do we love a weekend date like that so much? It tells us so many wonderful things about you. We like to watch you dry your hair and love the way you look in your bathrobe. It's fun to see how you get dressed in the morning and imperative that we know which section of the paper you read first. No doubt, staying over at our place for the first time is also a real journey of discovery for you. You can find out where we stuff our dirty laundry, whether or not we own two sets of sheets, and how early on a Saturday morning our mother calls to see if we had a date the night before.

A first weekend together can be equally as romantic if it takes place away from home, but there are a few more potential stumbling blocks. Since you're forced to really get to know one another in many intimate ways on a trip, it is always wise to consider all the details of the getaway, and ask questions if you have any doubts.

For starters, when a man invites you away for the weekend, he assumes it is implicitly (if not explicitly) understood that you are going to sleep with him. We don't book a room in a charming hotel, inn, or lodge unless we think you're going to share a bed with us. So if you agree to go, and he has not yet made love to you, be prepared for advances to be made very shortly after check-in. Of course, this isn't a dire threat. You don't *have* to do anything you don't want to do—although you may want to make your wants and needs clear ahead of time. But please note, we will be hoping to at least get into some serious smooching by a roaring fireplace and snuggling in bed, even if it is through your favorite thick and woolly flannel pajamas.

More likely, by the time we escape for our first weekend together we'll already be lovers, and the new territory we'll be crossing has to do with traveling as a couple. This seemingly innocuous activity can have more than romantic repercussions and needs to be undertaken with an open mind and a lot of patience. We've not yet spent this much uninterrupted time together, nor have we done so many intensely personal things in shared quarters. Brushing teeth, taking showers, eating meal after meal together with absolutely no escape. If you're thinking that doesn't sound the least bit romantic, you're right. The point here is to be realistic. In between walking in the woods or schussing down the slopes or lounging by the poolside, we have to deal with new things like sharing oodles of free time and personal space. This is very important stuff in a blossoming relationship.

When you find yourself on your first long weekend with a new beau, the best piece of advice for you (and for us) as a couple is to expect as little as possible and laugh as much as you can. When the car breaks down on our drive to Vermont, don't have a cow. Lots of fun and really good sex has been had in roadside motels all over America. (Did you think they installed those magic fingers for traveling salesmen?)

If the activity-filled island resort hotel turns out to have two leaky rowboats and a cracked, pavement tennis court, try not to write off the whole weekend as a disaster, and definitely don't act like a spoiled child. It's a lot more fun to just switch hotels, or find the best alternative beach on the island and make do. We don't plan these holiday surprises or disappointments. Sometimes potentially perfect weekends just turn into perfectly real travel nightmares.

Remember: we asked you on this date because we wanted to be with *you*. We hope all the details fall into place, but if there are a few snafus along the way, please help us make the best of the situation. Not only will we both be laughing about it at work on Monday morning, but your new boyfriend will have a great impression of how resilient you are, which says everything about the girlfriend he hopes you will be.

A Few Romantic Weekend Getaways You Might Not Have Tried Yet

- Monterey, California
- Chesapeake Bay, Maryland
- A sleeper car on a cross country train
- San Antonio, Texas
- Montreal, Canada
- Whitefish, Montana
- 500 miles of *any* two-lane highway in the U.S.
- Santa Fe, New Mexico
- The Hamptons, Long Island, in the *winter*
- Bar Harbor, Maine

THE FAMILY AFFAIR

You love his smile. And his thick wavy hair. The way he winks at you from across the office. And the boyish look he gets when he's snoring on your pillow with sunlight from the bedroom window streaming down onto his naked chest. You're completely smitten. Then one night over dinner, his voice takes on a serious undertone, something you've never heard before. "I've got something to tell you," he confides as the look in his eyes sends a shiver of fear up your spine. You've been sleeping with this man for two months. What can he possibly have to say of such gravity? He takes your hand, squeezes it, and blurts out: "My mother invited us to dinner!"

Warning sirens go off in your brain. You've got to meet his parents. The wonderful man you're falling in love with actually comes from somewhere. He is the product of two people. Do you really want to know that much about him yet? Do you want to see his father's paunch and bask in his mother's pride and spend a long evening being assessed by two people who are wondering: Can you possibly be good enough for their son? Unfortunately, you have no choice. This is a good time to give some real thought to how serious you are about this guy. Be sure you're *really* interested, because we never take you home to the folks unless we know that we like you. A lot! You're being given a golden opportunity to take stock *or* take a breather. Don't meet his folks unless you're pretty confident you want to notch your relationship to the next level.

If you should consent to this meeting, take a deep breath and buck up for what could be one of life's great challenges. You can count on receiving one of two responses. Either his family will regard you with surprisingly little interest, which should tell you that this man has brought home one too many girlfriends! Or they will enthusiastically welcome you into the bosom of their family before you even cross the threshold of their home, in which case you might as well start picking out china patterns. Why do we put you through this ordeal? Because short of buying you a ring, it is one of our subtle ways of saying, "I-I-I-guess I-I-like, uhh, I mean, uhhh—I love you."

On the other hand, should you be worried if we've been dating you for eons and the relationship is going great guns, but we *haven't* invited you to meet our family? Probably not. For some guys, that step just takes more time than others. Either count your blessings or turn the tables.

Invite him to meet *yours!* Don't be surprised though, if after you suggest this, he suddenly gets bogged down in one weekend project after another.

"Gotta go to the office on Sunday, honey." Or, "You know I told you I was going to paint all the moldings in the apartment this weekend!" Or our best and last resort: "Do you still want to go to that little bed and breakfast we've been talking about since we met? Just the *two* of us?"

Initially, we'll do anything to avoid the first meeting with your family. We're just as nervous about it as you are. However, once you have us roped into an actual date, we're generally very pliant. We might even be able to work up a little enthusiasm. Just tell us what to wear, how to behave, and who to avoid.

Actually, we don't mind meeting your folks all that much. They *are* your folks and we always enjoy seeing the prototype of what you will someday become! We'll just approach that first meeting with the same confident swagger we used to win your heart. So keeping that warning in mind, if you want a guy to know you really feel special about him, bring on Mom and Dad, your sister and twin brothers, Grandma and Grandpa, Aunt Ruth and Uncle Maury and the rest of the gang. We promise we'll be on our best behavior (except when we have our "cheerleader fantasy" flashback and try to make love to you on your old high school bed!).

Getting Along with the Guys

The parents are a filial responsibility. If we've been dating you long enough, the pressure from home will eventually compel us to meet one another's families whether either of us is ready or not. But then the folks are a piece of cake compared to meeting the friends. We're really not that concerned about what you think of Mom and Dad early in our relationship anyway. (We know you're going to lie and say you loved them until we're engaged or married, at which point you'll hit us with the awful truth!) A man's friends are a different matter, though. They are his most prized possession and he cares deeply about your reaction to them, and will be deeply swayed by how they feel about you. (Is this making you nervous yet?)

Some of our friends, in particular, the ones who are married or have longtime steady girlfriends, not only mean the world to us, but also represent a fantasy—that we would someday become a member of the "taken" club too. If he invites you out with the married-with-children group, then you know he sees a real future.

When Keith, a 35-year-old bachelor, finally got into a long-term relationship with Janine, he kept her from his gang for the longest time. Finally Janine asked him: "Why don't we ever do something with your pals? Is there something wrong?" Keith confided that because all of his friends were married and most had kids, he was worried that she'd be intimidated by them. He didn't want to scare her off by subjecting her to their little world of domestic bliss too early in their relationship. But Janine was game, and organized a dinner party at Keith's house, inviting three married couples. For

Keith, it proved to be the most satisfying moment in his relationship with Janine to date. When he walked out of his kitchen carrying a meticulously wrought cassoulet, to find his new girlfriend comfortably ensconced in conversation with his best buddies and their wives, he nearly got tears in his eyes. Getting along with our friends is one of the great votes of confidence you can give us.

You don't have to change, perform, or put on a show the first time you meet the gang. Since they have already heard a ton about you (far more than you'd ever want them to), we know they're going to like you. So you can pretty much be yourself—with a little extra tolerance and humor perhaps. We're far more worried about what *you* are going to think of *them,* especially those guy friends who have a tendency to be a little, well, over the top.

Naturally, we'll want to meet *your* friends as well, and we may start to get a little antsy if you don't introduce us after a while. We'll wonder if there's something wrong with our relationship, or whether we somehow embarrass you. Introducing us to your gang reassures us that you're also in this affair for the long run.

When You Meet the Guys

DON'T	DO
Overcompensate by doing tequila shooters and telling X-rated jokes to impress them.	Share your vast knowledge of sports. Drop a few names. Show them you really know your stuff.

DON'T	DO
Get into a screaming match if one of them baits you with some dopey "guy" comment.	Match the tough ones blow for blow with your witty repartee.
Feel like you have to give a testimonial on how wonderful your boyfriend is.	Make the extra effort with his best friend. He'll end up being one of your best pals, too.

When Is It Time to Share Drawers?

Tom, a New York television executive, had been dating Sheila for almost a year when he left on a three-week business trip to Asia. Perhaps it was the thirteen-hour time difference that made her feel so far away to him. Or maybe it was the fear that crept into his heart when he thought about the things his extremely attractive girlfriend could be doing while he was out of touch in Hong Kong, Bangkok, and Singapore. For all he knew, it was something they put in his tea while he held business meetings in China. But when Tom returned home exhausted from a twenty-two-hour flight, the first thing he did was ask Sheila if she'd consider living with him. A month later they moved in together.

There are plenty of great reasons to contemplate living with your boyfriend. And there are a few surefire ways to blow the whole affair before you ever get there. Plenty of men think of a live-in relationship as a dry run to marriage. We like the idea of "playing house." But it is definitely one area where you don't want to move too fast. In a budding relationship, it's best to take baby steps towards the larger commitment of cohabitation, because it can be just as difficult and traumatic to get out of a live-in relationship as a marriage.

In working toward the possibility of living together, you'll start out on the right foot by using sleepover etiquette on your weekends together. Remember how you used to ask, "Hey Ma, can I sleep over at Jamie's?" And Mom always said, *"Were you invited?"* Well, weekend romances work best when we both keep that question in mind. We have no right to plant our toothbrush in your toothbrush holder unless you invite us to. That may be more commitment than you're ready for, or you may have someone else who occasionally brushes his teeth in your bathroom. (And believe me, we look in your medicine cabinet probably as often as you do ours!)

Okay, now let's say that you and your boyfriend have spent every weekend together for the past two months. You even stay together on weeknights once in a while. And you mostly do this at his place. At this point, it seems perfectly logical and practical for him to clear a spot in his dresser for you to throw a few pairs of underwear. You're starting to feel silly carrying clean panties and a bra in your briefcase to work every day just in case you end up spending the night with him. That drawer of undies doesn't seem like a big deal to you. However, to a man in a new relationship, it's the equivalent of giving you an engagement ring.

We know women find this notion ridiculous. "Grow up," you say. "It's just a couple pairs of undies." But please try to understand. We love you. We love being with you. We even love the speed at which our relationship is growing. But your asking for that drawer, or any other shared space, is tantamount to asking us to promise we're never going to sleep with another woman again for the rest of our lives. "Foul!" you cry. "If you're seeing another woman, screw you!" Which brings me to the truth about guys.

We are *not* seeing another woman. We don't want to see another woman. But somewhere between the time we met you and the time we first slept with you—and now—we want to *think* we could see another woman. We're not actually going to do it, and we're not barring you from the underwear drawer because we hope to "do it."

The drawer is symbolic. Even if we are committed to you in our hearts, minds, and bodies, there is still a part of us—our egos perhaps—that is taking a little longer to accept the fact that by dating you we aren't going to have any other weekend guests! You don't have to put up with this attitude for ten months or three years. All we're asking for is a bit of patience in the beginning. Don't lean on us about that underwear drawer too quickly. We'll get there—once we've adjusted to our newfound monogamy.

Of course, if we seem to be taking too long, there are plenty of tantalizing ways to speed up the male maturing process. If you really want to put your man to the test (and don't try this unless you know him well enough to trust him), here's a suggestion.

On one of those Saturday afternoons when he's expecting you to hang out with him all weekend, surprise him. Pluck yourself from the couch and go take a shower. Repack your stuff and go home. Not angrily. Not with malice. Just tell him you have plans for the evening that don't include him. If he asks, tell him you're going out with your friends. Tell him he's got a free pass for Saturday night out with his buddies now. Then kiss him goodbye and leave him his valuable "space." Don't stay out all night. Positively don't do anything stupid. This is not a suggestion to go cheat. It's simply an opportunity for him to appreciate what he's got.

You see, while he's out drinking beer with the boys for the first time in three months, he's bound to spend some time wondering where you are and what you're doing and with whom. Within a couple of hours, he'll probably be thinking about how good you looked when you left his apartment—and how good you'd look to a city full of still-single men!

After you've given him his "space" for a few hours, drag your gang to the bar he and his buddies hang out at. Join them and have a blast, all of you together. Rest assured he'll be thrilled to see you. Give him time for one last beer with his buds, then kidnap him, drag him to your place like it's a first date, and make love to him like there's no tomorrow. Make it steamy. Make it memorable. And make him remember why he fell in love with you in the first place. It's amazing what a little fear and a little refresher course will do for a man on the cusp of commitment. That underwear drawer may be yours sooner than you think!